D1612764

OH, REF!

OH, REF!

Pat Partridge
and
John Gibson

READERS UNION
Group of Book Clubs
Newton Abbot 1980

This book has been made possible by the forbearance and tolerance of Margaret over the years. She has helped to make everything in my career possible.

Pat P.

Acknowledgements

Photographs by courtesy of Peter Robinson, Newcastle Chronicle and Journal Ltd, North of England Newspapers, Middlesbrough Evening Gazette, Daily Mail, Daily Express, Harry Ormesher; also for the help from the Eccles and District Referees Association.

Contents

Foreword by Alan Hardaker O.B.E.
General Secretary Football League

It is a great pleasure for me to write a foreword to the story of Pat Partridge's career as a referee.

It is generally accepted that the North-East is a breeding ground for footballers, but it may, perhaps, not be generally known that it has also produced over the years many of our outstanding Officials. It is no exaggeration to say that Pat has added his name to that list with distinction.

He joined The League in 1965-66 as a Linesman, and was promoted to Referee in 1966-67 Season. In all that time Pat has had an outstanding record and has never had anything but a successful season in all his career as a Football League Referee.

He has achieved all the honours that it is possible for a referee to achieve and there is no doubt that anyone interested in the refereeing side of the game must be intrigued by the story of his experiences.

I would not like to say that Pat Partridge has never had a game when he might have thought to himself that, looking back, he might have refereed a little bit better. This happens to all referees at some time in their career, but the successful ones learn from that experience and, as a consequence, it does not happen very often. I think the secret of Pat's success has been mainly due to the fact that, when he has had a game in which controversial decisions have been made, he has never, to my knowledge, ever tried to justify himself – which is the mistake that many referees make.

He has always taken the attitude that he has refereed the game honestly, given decisions on what he himself has seen and he has never allowed himself to be ruffled by television inquests, press inquests, or unenlightened criticism.

He has refereed all over the world in every important competition, and I am sure that this book will be read not only by budding referees, but by football enthusiasts inside and outside the game.

A Hardaker

Introduction

Pat Partridge is England's undisputed top referee – a position officially recognised last year when he was selected as his country's sole representative on the FIFA panel for the World Cup finals in Argentina. But his appointment in fact went much, much further than that. It formally confirmed what everyone had until then privately recognised and that was his position as one of the world's greatest referees. Possibly even the greatest.

It was the supreme accolade bestowed on a man who has risen to the pinnacle of a profession he only entered because of continual bullying from two of his work mates.

Partridge was accepted onto the Football League referees list in 1966 and a meteoric rise through the ranks to senior FIFA rating has seen him handle top games all over the world . . . behind the Iron Curtain, in virtually every European country, in the Middle East, Brazil, Argentina, Japan and even India.

His pedigree is impressive in the extreme. He has officiated in no fewer than five Wembley cup finals of various colours from running the line in the 1971 European Cup final to taking the middle for our two prestige national finals, the FA Cup and Football League Cup. He has also refereed the SV Hamburg–Anderlecht European Cupwinners' Cup final two years ago and the Cruzeiro–Bayern Munich World Club Championship match of 1976 in South America.

Pat Partridge has rightly been described as a person who has walked into some of football's biggest trouble spots with the air of a pin-striped diplomat rather than the defiance of a man off a gun boat.

If we have the best referees in the world, which is a generally regarded fact, then he epitomises all that is admirable in our officials wielding authority without brandishing it like a cudgel.

His philosophy is 'to talk to players man to man rather than teacher to pupil or even father to son. He doesn't swear because he sees no need to and says if he had to gain respect that way he would quit but he readily recognises the existence of soccer's industrial language.

An unobtrusive law enforcer on the field, he is also a law enforcer off it having become a Justice of the Peace a few months ago.

His passion for football is all consuming. If he hasn't a League game in the cauldron of Anfield or Old Trafford Partridge, who with his brother-in-law Stuart runs a dairy farm perched high in the south Durham hillsides, will go down into the tiny village of Cockfield and ref the local pub side.

'I hate Saturdays off. I'd rather pay people overtime and take a village game than stay at home. It's that sort of gut feeling which distinguishes the referee from all the other breeds. Money doesn't come into it. If it did I would never have blown a whistle in my life. There are no fortunes to be made for the men in black.'

Even so the fanaticism of Partridge is renowned throughout the game. He is known to the players as the ref who never turns down a testimonial match. On the Monday after taking charge of the 1975 FA Cup final between West Ham and Fulham in front of 100,000 people at Wembley he refereed a benefit match in the North West Durham steel town of Consett when 984 folk turned up in blinding rain and he was the biggest name on the programme.

No one, not even an outsider, could fail to recognise the extent that football dominates the lifestyle of Pat Partridge and his wife Margaret. Their house is called Law One, the family cars are REF 1 and REF 47 (referees must retire at the age of 47) and, after he returned from the World Cup finals, Margaret bought him a frisky black labrador which was registered at the Kennel Club under the name Argentina Mundial. Tina to you and me.

But if his den is a personal treasure trove of pennants, inscribed tankards, medals, ornaments and books recording every solitary match he has ever handled at any level, it would be totally wrong to presume that the man is all surface.

Partridge has, as an administrator and referee supremo, made a deep and lasting impression on the game he loves.

He and Sir Stanley Rous are the only two referees to take the FA Cup final and be president of the Association of Football League Referees and Linesmen in the same season and it is from such a strong platform that Partridge has campaigned loud and long for much greater liaison between the players and referees.

The need to weld together the Association of Football League Referees and Linesmen and the PFA, and even to bring in Supporters Clubs as well, to help everyone understand the on-field problems of the present-day game is Pat Partridge's particular hobby-horse.

He states his case forcibly. 'I'm a firm believer that a lot of the trouble we see at football grounds these days is a direct result of an "us and them" attitude. Some referees think they are above players and equally a lot of players believe refs are incompetent amateurs. There is a dire need for the two parties to mix off the park because it's the players and referees, not the managers, administrators or coaches, who matter on a Saturday afternoon.

'They hold the stage between three o'clock and twenty to five and the whole show depends almost entirely on their ability to communicate.'

Happily those sentiments have, as a direct result of unstinting work by Partridge and other caring men, borne fruit recently. A series of meetings between the Association of Football League Referees and Linesmen and PFA have taken place though much more ground is still to be covered before the necessary bond is fully established.

The story of Pat Partridge provides the reader with a unique look behind the scenes and introduces him to perhaps the most misunderstood man in football . . . the man in the middle.

Pat is due to retire next year but he was determined to voice his forthright opinions on a wide range of topics while he was still in the game rather than after leaving it.

In revealing his innermost thoughts and dealings with the great names of football, not just in this country but abroad, it is possible that a new light will be thrown on the men whose parentage is traditionally questioned each and every Saturday. That alone would make everything worthwhile.

1 'Think it but never say it'

If I possess some of the essential ingredients of a good referee, such as an inbred sense of discipline and a steeliness not to shirk the unpleasant decisions of life, then I owe them directly to my father. I have even taken his full name Patrick Partridge.

He was born on the banks of the Tyne at the turn of the century in those sombre days when poverty was a constant companion in the North East and consequently decided that the only course of action open to him if he were to escape the dole queues was to run away and join the Army. This he did giving a false age to overcome the fact that he was too young for the life of a soldier.

In all my father was to serve 22 years as a professional soldier split into two parts, the first after signing on as a boy and the second during World War Two. In between times, now married, he moved to Billingham to work at the giant ICI plant and I was introduced to the world.

My father has always remained, however, an Army man through and through. He was a strict disciplinarian, master in his own home, his word law not to be challenged. Yet never once did he raise his hand to me. A stern word was enough or, if he was not present, the threat to tell my father I was out of line. I learned the value of discipline from his example at an early age and I have grown to respect him immensely. His military mind told him that the body also needed to be tuned if the brain were to work to full capacity and if he enjoyed a night of drinking in the mess then the following morning would see him in the gymnasium working it off.

I always remember my father giving me the best piece of advice I have ever received. It was offered as I was about to be introduced to military life myself for the two years of my national service and it was: 'Think it but never say it.' That has been my yardstick ever since and it is so applicable to the world of soccer that I wish many, many more fathers had told it to their sons before they grew up to be professional footballers. It would have made my job now so much more easy.

'Think it but never say it' has become my theme whenever I address referees' societies though I must admit that on one occasion when those words were taken literally on the field of play my ace was trumped.

'Referee, what would you do if I called you a bastard?' one player inquired politely. 'I'd send you off,' I replied. 'What would you do if I thought you were a bastard?' was the next question. 'There's not a lot I could do,' I answered. 'In that case, ref, I think you're a bastard,' he said turning smartly on his heel.

Despite the certain enterprise of that particular footballer I feel that, by and large, those words of my father's hold true. He is a remarkable man totally belying his birthdate – April Fool's Day – and was actually awarded the MBE though to this very day I don't know precisely what for. Whenever I've asked him his reply has been the same. 'For doing my job properly,' he would say.

It was to have been a great day for the Partridge family when my father was to get his medal from the old king, George VI, at Buckingham Palace during the war years. I was 10 years of age and was to travel to London with my mother for the ceremony but my father's regiment was going on a mission and consequently the whole thing had to be done rather quickly which meant mam and I missing out. The immense disappointment stayed with me for a long time.

My mother, Catherine, is a gentle lady to whom nothing is a burden. She still takes old folk's dogs out for a walk if the snow is thick despite the fact that I tell her she herself might now qualify for any such help going the way of the elderly.

The family home when I first drew breath on June 30, 1933 was 37 St Vincent Street, a row of terraced houses in Haverton Hill, Billingham. I don't know whether it was the shock of first clapping eyes on me or merely by choice but I've remained the only offspring of Patrick and Catherine Partridge.

We stayed at Haverton Hill for only a matter of months before moving across Billingham to a much more expansive and pleasant house newly built at Cowpen. It was a spruce semi-detached in Bedford Terrace with acres of welcome grassland surrounding it and my parents still live happily there.

The fields were paradise to me and a permanent source of dirty clothes to my mother. Football was second only to breathing and daily I returned, as we Geordies would say, covered from head to toes in clarts from my exertions with a tennis ball.

My formal education began at St John's School less than a mile from our home and was, at first at least, a welcome extension to my life. Before I was allowed through the gates at the age of five I was often to be found peering longingly at the other boys and girls enjoying the pleasures of education. Frankly I can't recollect being so enthusiastic once those gates were flung open to me for the greater part of the next decade.

Though not a dunce I didn't exactly excel academically failing to pass my 11-plus examination and I remained at St John's until leaving age when I moved to the technical college in Stockton with aspirations of becoming 'something in engineering'.

My father came home from the war in 1945 and his return marked my introduction to a soccer ground which has, even with my later professional introduction to the inside of all the world's great football stadiums, remained closest to my heart. Ayresome Park, home of Middlesbrough AFC.

I was 12 years of age, impressionable as all kids are as they prepare to enter their teens, and ready to commit my soul to the Boro. The journey from our house to Ayresome, something like six miles all in, was an adventure in itself. Dad and I would get a bus from home down to the Transporter Bridge which would then ferry us across the Tees and then another bus up to Ayresome. I can still remember the excitement of that final penny ride as we got closer to the football ground and the streets swelled with happy faces, red scarfs and the incessant buzz of men and boys discussing the impending heroics of their favourites.

Boro, to me, were the cream. I kept a scrapbook recording their every achievement and was immensely proud of the team. Rightly so, I believe, because there was no other club in the country which provided two players in the Great Britain side against the Rest of Europe as Boro did. Full-back George Hardwick was Britain's captain and the Golden Boy himself, Wilf Mannion, played inside-forward.

The names were magic to a boy . . . Hardwick, Mannion, Micky Fenton at centre-forward, Dickie Robinson, Harry Bell, and a goalkeeper called Dave Cumming. I was standing immediately behind Cumming's goal on the afternoon Boro were playing Arsenal and he got a bit sick of Leslie

Compton. Out of the blue Cumming clipped Compton a pearler on the chin, whipped his jersey over his head in disgust, and walked off the field. He never even waited for the referee to instruct an early bath and, if my memory serves me right, no disciplinary action was ever taken his previous record was so exemplary.

In adult life I have remained close to Middlesbrough Football Club often being called upon to give lectures to their players on the understanding needed between referees and players and, if ever I have needed treatment for injuries, their facilities have always been available. Consequently even when I moved away from Teesside I felt too involved at Ayresome to ever take their matches and I contacted the Football League to request that I should never be asked to officiate at one of their games. That has been the case throughout my career barring, of course, pre-season friendlies and testimonials and even then Boro's players have always maintained that they hated me in the middle because I bend over backwards to be ultra fair to the other side just to prove my impartiality.

While making my regular pilgrimages to Ayresome Park I was also playing for my school team St John's and later Billingham Synthonia Juniors minor team (14 to 16 age group) and junior side (16 to 18). The Synthonia teams were part of the ICI set up and as my father worked there I sneaked membership that way.

My playing career went backwards – literally. I began as an outside-right, went to wing-half, and finished up at full-back. I would like to think I was versatile but perhaps it would be nearer the mark to say I would play anywhere for a game.

In minor football we once went a full season undefeated which was something an alert ICI official remembered when I went to Argentina to referee in the World Cup finals because he dug out the old team photograph and printed it in the works magazine.

One of my arch rivals on the field and firm friend off it was Barry Butler who went on to play professional football for Norwich City as a centre-half. He was with Stockton West End, a big lad who also stood out head and shoulders above the rest of us on talent. We used to go to night school together and sample the delights of Saturday night dances.

The year I got on the Football League line – 1965 – I was given the Huddersfield v Norwich City match and decided to surprise Barry who as far as I was aware didn't know I had 'made it' in football as well. I certainly had not told him since he moved away and unless he had read of it, which was extremely unlikely in East Anglia, he was ignorant of my new status in life.

When I arrived at the ground I noticed that Barry was missing from the Norwich team and I asked their manager Ron Ashman why. He explained that Barry had been injured and was easing his way back. My reunion was not to be that day or any other. That self same night Barry was killed in a car crash.

The general wear and tear of playing football pushed me out of one facet of the game and into another. By the age of 18 I was attending the Stockton and Thornaby Hospital on a regular basis in an effort to strengthen the damaged tendons in both my ankles. The trouble was not the result of one particular incident but rather the accumulated effects of several hard games.

Anyway my playing days were over apart from the odd game now and again. By this time I was a working man serving my time as an electrician with Head Wrightson, an engineering firm in Thornaby.

Alec Brown and Harry Bage both worked for the same company and over the next couple of years they niggled

away at me to take up refereeing. Alec was a Football
League ref and Harry officiated in the North Eastern League
and the joys of being a man in the middle were repeatedly
laid temptingly before me. Resistance came easily at first
but the Chinese torture of constantly dripping ice cold water
onto a shaved head is, they say, guaranteed to bring the
desired effect in time. It took two years for me to succumb.
To Alec and Harry I say a sincere 'thank you' for their
persistence without which I would never have been writing
this book today.

The referees' coaching course was being held in Stockton
YMCA, not the most glamorous of places, with a chap called
Jimmy Eden putting us through our six sessions at the end
of which Durham Football Association council members
trooped down to our headquarters to eye the finished
product.

It will probably come as a source of genuine amazement
to an outsider to be told that you become a referee sitting
round a table in a youth hostel reading books or chalking
on a blackboard without ever getting onto a pitch with 22
players. There is no practical side to the exam at all. But in
fact a piece of paper doesn't make a referee. All it means is
that you know the laws of the game and you become a
Class Three referee which limits you to junior and minor
football which is where you get the practical experience you
require.

I know of no superior way of introducing an enthusiast to
the refereeing profession and throughout my career I have
found that those who knock the system from its inception
up to FIFA standing are people who have not made the
progress they expected.

Be that as it may the momentous day Pat Partridge was
let loose with a whistle in his hand to wreak havoc on our
national sport was February 24, 1953 – a Tuesday.

My certificate which I still have reads:

> This is to certify that Mr Patrick Partridge
> 8 Bedford Terrace, Billingham, County Durham
> passed an examination held by the referee's committee at
> YMCA Stockton-on-Tees on 24 Feb 1953
> and is now duly registered as a referee with the Durham
> County Football Association.
>
> J B Blenkinsopp, secretary.
> Fred Hall, chairman.

In the top left hand corner it had written in pen 'Junior Football only.'

That certificate from Jim Blenkinsopp is the only referee's certificate I have ever received. I'm still waiting for my senior one and if I ever get it I'll really go places!

I was almost 20 years old and at that time in Durham any referee under the age of 21 was restricted to taking charge of matches involving players 18 and under – a rule now changed incidentally.

Such was the help I received at Head Wrightson first from Alec Brown and Harry Bage and then Jimmy Dickinson that a football match was promptly arranged for the following Saturday, especially for my benefit, four days after passing my exam. Jimmy Dickinson, of course, is a famous footballing name though I rather think this particular JD had a much more basic vocabulary than the Portsmouth and England wing-half. The heart, however, was pure gold. Being secretary of the football section Jimmy was able to arrange for the second team, which had a free day, to play another works side in a friendly match.

On the Friday afternoon prior to the game I asked my boss if I could slip out for an hour and I hared down to the local sports outfitters to buy my referee's attire. I had been told from the outset 'Look the part and you're halfway there.' I turned out in the full black regalia and black canvas hockey boots.

The match itself was uneventful. I received no bother from the players which was hardly surprising as it was a friendly. I was of secondary importance to the pleasure of a kickabout and they did not bother about me. After that I handled matches in the 14 to 16 age group and as I was a few years older I seemed accepted. I strongly believe, however, that kids in those days respected authority much more than they do now.

My first official game was on March 7 when I was in charge of the West End v Billingham Swifts match in the Stockton and District Junior League. I was paid the princely sum of three shillings and six pence for my efforts and a referee's monetary lot has not improved that much over the years. I now receive £25 for handling a Football League match though I hasten to add I am not complaining. It isn't the pocket but the heart which is our driving force.

That season, 1952–53, I took 11 games, running the line once. How, you might wonder, have I such a memory for precise detail. The truth is that for some reason I do not quite know I entered details of my first game as a referee in a hard backed exercise book and I have continued to enter the date, teams, league and result of every solitary game I have ever been involved in to this day. I believe that by accident I must have the most comprehensive records of any referee in the world.

There is an amusing story attached to one of my earliest games in March of '53 between West End and Synthonia B played at Potato Hall, a farmer's field in Stockton. I had to abandon the match after 46 minutes with West End leading 2–0 when the ball struck a hawthorn hedge and burst. As there wasn't another ball to be had we could not continue.

It was the first and last time I was to face such hazards that even Anfield or Maine Road have never been able to equal!

People have often said to me that if I were to fall in the River Tees I would come up with a trout in my mouth I am that lucky and metaphorically speaking that was the case when, a month after becoming a fully fledged referee, I attended the March meeting of the Stockton Referees Association. At least I came up with a Cup final ticket if not a trout.

An item late on the agenda was the draw for two Wembley tickets and, lo and behold, I won one of them and a little later duly set out on the cattletruck, the midnight soccer special, for London and the final. What a feast was to be served up for this was to become known as the Matthews final when the great man at last got the only medal to elude him – a Cup winner's.

I had never seen Matthews play until that day. He had never turned out at Ayresome when I was on the terraces as a schoolboy and he mesmerised Bolton as Blackpool came back from the dead to win a breathtaking game 4-3 though it must be said that, in the euphoria of Matthews' achievement at long last, the performance of Stan Mortensen in scoring a hat-trick was somewhat forgotten.

Before I departed for London Harry Bage told me: 'Watch the referee, son.' He was Mervyn Griffiths and I thought he had a tremendous game. I must have been just about the only bloke in the 100,000 crowd at the Matthews final who could not take his eyes off the ref!

There was to be one more season for me in 1953–54 before my life was radically changed. During it I had 40 games (38 as referee and two as linesman) and had my first taste of officiating in finals being awarded the Stockton Minor Cup final ahead of our senior referee. Stockton Ex-Schoolboys beat Stockton West End 8–1.

Then on my 21st birthday an invitation from Her Majesty's Government to join the armed forces dropped through the letterbox with my cards.

2 It's all Chinese

National Service to me meant two pleasant years when I could exercise my mind to the limit dreaming up various legitimate dodges to divert me from playing soldiers.

Sport turned out to be an ideal ploy. Not only did I enter the Army as a Class Three referee but a more than adequate water polo player as well and I went on to become a crack shot with the unit rifle team, a basketball player, hockey participant, and even volunteered for court hockey, that masochistic game played on a concrete pitch with a wall all the way round it so that the ball is never out of play. The only thing I never tried was rugby.

My ability as a swimmer stemmed from my early teens when my father took me to the baths which were only 100 yards from our school. He found me on the first day under the hot shower instead of in the pool and was disgusted to think I was scared of the water. I ended up going swimming at seven o'clock in the morning, at lunchtime, and at night four or five times a week.

By the time I was called up and told to report to Blandford in Dorset I was playing water polo for Billingham Synthonia and considered something of a key member of the side. Water polo had become my participant sport as a player following the injuries to my ankles and, frankly, I was probably more keen to tackle the water than I had been to tackle some big hairy winger in full flight.

I even got a 72-hour pass during my six-week basic

training, something virtually unheard of, as a result of my aspirations as a water polo player. It all came about through a neat dovetailing of events. I had suggested to my club, Synthonia, that they write to my commanding officer to request my release for the final of the Northumberland and Durham championships for which we had qualified. My suggestion was more in hope than expectancy I might add.

At the same time fate took a hand in Blandford when my unit was told: 'Anyone with swimming trunks fall in. We're going to a pool in Poole.' I was in line like a shot and when during the session someone threw a water polo ball in amongst us I was in seventh heaven and my natural ability duly noted.

That little incident coincided with the arrival of a letter from Billingham and, much to my surprise, I was informed that as I was making satisfactory progress as a soldier I could have a 72-hour pass to play in the finals. We lost but it was still a worthwhile exercise.

The first of Partridge's sporting sidetracks had worked a treat but I must stress that while I was always ready to try something out I took soldiering seriously inasmuch as I was never going to let my father down. He was a military man and there was no danger of his son dishonouring him though, equally, there was no danger of my following in his footsteps by making the Army my profession. I was actually approached to do so because I did my job properly but I politely refused.

From Blandford it was on to Malvern for a 12-week electrical course where one of the first sights on arrival at the camp was a notice pinned on the board announcing a referee's course. There had been no time for refereeing during my basic training but now it was different. My commander, Major Mallen, was involved in Army football circles and when I informed him that I was a qualified referee I was automatically made an Army Class Three ref which saw me handling both services and local football.

A dear and lasting friendship sprang from my short stay here or, to be more precise, from a routine inspection carried out by a second lieutenant John Boyne. He spotted a referee's kit, neatly ironed and spruced, hanging behind the locker door and asked: 'What's this?' When I explained he took a closer look and saw the words 'Durham county' on the breast pocket badge. 'Where precisely in Durham?' he inquired and when I told him Billingham it turned out that his home was actually three quarters of a mile from mine. From that day on I had a friend, the sort who once gave me his boots to go on guard duty when I returned from leave less than adequately equipped.

John is now a brigadier at the age of 44 and whenever I take a match in London he is my guest. A super fellow.

My next port of call was Hong Kong where I was to see out the remainder of my time as a National Serviceman. I volunteered to be shipped abroad rather than run the risk of being posted to Catterick. It would have broken my heart to have been so close to home without being able to make it.

Such a decision made me a League referee in one fell swoop though it must be stated in the interest of accuracy that while I was to officiate in the Hong Kong League from my moment of arrival it was little more than parkland standard and not to be compared to our structure in this country.

I was registered with the Hong Kong FA as a Class Three referee which allowed me to take charge of Third or Fourth Division matches. Hong Kong is, as you know, a small island and consequently has limited playing areas. The First and Second Division clubs have their own stadiums but the Third and Fourth play in a unique setting in Happy Valley.

Let me explain. Happy Valley is a huge, beautiful race-course, oval in shape with numerous soccer pitches in the middle of it. Often between eighteen and twenty matches take place at once with a full race meeting going on at the same time. The horses don't seem to mind the distraction and the spectators in the stand can choose their football match to watch in between races.

The games are played over the weekends with staggered kick offs. Each pitch is used twice on a Saturday and three times on a Sunday when the schoolboys join in yet, because of the dry weather, they remain surprisingly good.

We were stationed at Victoria Barracks a tram ride away from Happy Valley where in mid November of 1955 I handled my first game, a Division Three match between Taikoo and Telephones which ended 2–2. We had kicked off early and as I left the pitch to go through the gate and over the racecourse to the dressing-rooms I was approached by two elderly Chinese gentlemen in full referee's regalia. One stopped me and asked if I would mind lending a helping hand with their match which was just about to begin as part of the 'backshift.'

'Not at all, I'll run the line,' I replied but they insisted that I act as referee so on I went again to complete a three-hour non-stop stint. It was just as well I was supremely fit through being an Army man.

Hollandia, a Dutch settlement team, beat Lane Crawfords 2–0 but during the game I had to send off two players. Back in the dressing-room one of my Chinese linesmen turned to me and said: 'You were perfectly correct to order off those two. One was my son. Now you realise why we wanted you to referee. We were both involved through our families.'

League games on the island brought referees like myself a

small match fee but the schoolboy games on a Sunday morning were run on a purely voluntary basis. However my love for football was such that I happily refereed whenever possible and at the end of the season we who had offered our services were rewarded by the Hong Kong Schools FA who threw a lavish banquet – and I do mean lavish – at which we were each presented with a solid silver engraved whistle. It has remained one of my proudest possessions.

Schools soccer honoured me further the following April, two months after I had been promoted to a Class Two referee, when I ran the line in the Hong Kong-Manila schoolboy international. The other linesman and the referee were both Chinese.

The 17 months I spent in Hong Kong were, as I have said, extremely happy but there was one episode which marred my stay. It produced my one and only brush with authority in the shape of my commanding officer, a man who made such a lasting impression on me that I cannot even remember his name.

I had been appointed by the Army FA to take charge of one of the Major Units Challenge Cup semi-finals on the same day as my own unit, the District Workshops, was to play in the Minor Units semi-final. I turned out occasionally for our mob as a player but never on a regular basis. The invitation to whistle the big cup-tie had been made and accepted several weeks previously but the day before the two games I was pulled up by one of our staff sergeants and asked if I were playing. 'I can't, Staff. I'm refereeing the Major Units semi tomorrow,' I told him which seemed satisfactory enough to all concerned. However ten minutes later the door burst open and the same staff sergeant barked: 'The Old Man wants to see you, Partridge. Get your cap on and get up that yard double quick.'

As soon as I walked in the CO said: 'I understand you have refused to play for the unit tomorrow.' I was flabbergasted. That was, of course, completely untrue but I was unable to get a word in edgeways to explain. He ranted on incessantly lecturing me about loyalty, comradeship and virtually everything he could possibly drag into a distinctly one-sided argument. During it all my father's piece of advice 'Think it but never say it' flashed before my mind and it was probably just as well. Had I been able to speak freely at that moment I would probably have been thrown in the harbour.

Eventually I managed to explain that I was unable to play because the only body which could release me from refereeing the senior semi-final was the Army FA. This brought no abatement merely the lifting of a telephone and a call to Major Walker demanding: 'What's this Mickey?'

The outcome after some considerable to-ing and fro-ing was that I was instructed to play in the first game and referee the second, an extremely unsatisfactory state of affairs made possible by the staggered kick-offs.

I felt that I could hardly give my all mentally as well as physically to two such important cup semi-finals within a couple of hours of each other. One step from a final appearance means a tremendous amount to all teams. It is a one-off, now-or-never situation which is considerably different to the Third or Fourth Division matches I had refereed in a day.

I played in the first game and we were beaten. Normally I go out to win whatever I am doing but this time I found it impossible. I had been ordered to do something which was a hobby and I was unable to respond in the normal way. The CO had done no one a favour with his heavy handed attitude including himself.

Water polo produced no such pulling of rank. The very

opposite was the case in fact. I was merely a craftsman yet I captained the Army team which included majors and other superiors. When I said jump they jumped – in the water. The Chinese are expert water polo players but we were pretty warm ourselves and we actually became the first Army side to win the Colonial Cup which was quite something.

Although a centre-half I always scored a fair number of goals and I managed to grab a couple in the final. Swimming generally was my forte outside of refereeing and I also won the junior 440 yards freestyle title at the Colony Swimming and Diving championships receiving quite a bit of Press coverage in the process. A report even filtered back to England and appeared in the local newspapers complete with photograph of me in uniform and beret. Mine were proud parents.

Demob was followed quickly by promotion as a referee for after only one season back in the district leagues around Teesside I was awarded my Class One status. It was 1957 and I was 24 years of age.

The route to the top was clearly defined in those days. The Central League was virtually a closed shop to us in the farthest northern corner of England because, with only one club in the competition, we were allowed only one referee and four linesmen on the list. Therefore the major stepping stone to the Football League was the North Eastern League, a good semi-pro competition with a fine mixture of teams. There were the reserve sides of Sunderland, Middlesbrough, Carlisle, Darlington and Hartlepool balanced against the likes of Blyth Spartans, South Shields, Ashington, Annfield Plain, West Stanley, Stockton, North Shields and Horden Colliery Welfare.

The North Eastern League was a tremendous grounding for young players who were given the opportunity to play against or alongside some of the old timers stepping down a grade yet Alan Brown, then manager of Sunderland, saw fit to cause its destruction.

He was the prime mover in the disbanding of the league because he felt the competition was not good enough for his reserve players and he found an ally in Middlesbrough. Together they made a futile attempt to form a north central league for the reserve sides of Football League clubs only and in the process killed off a competition which was a tradition.

I firmly believe that Alan Brown did North East football a great disservice with his actions and I would go as far as to say that non-league soccer in the area has never fully recovered. Certainly the selfish and short-sighted attitude of Brown struck deep at the hearts of the ambitious young referees in the North East who suddenly saw their lifeline to the Football League cut off and it was no coincidence that in the next five years after the North Eastern League was disbanded at the end of the season not one referee from the area was promoted to the League list.

It did not affect me because I had only just become a Class One referee and was still learning my trade lining and then refereeing in the strictly amateur Northern League but I saw some referees who were almost there have the door slammed firmly in their face never to open again. I wonder whether that aspect of his actions ever occurred to Alan Brown.

When my own breakthrough came it was totally unexpected if more than welcome. Before the start of the 1965–66 season the Football League and the Football Association decided that they wanted a new system for referees whereby more avenues were open throughout the country so they set up a chain of feeder and contributory leagues. In all there were to be 13 contributory leagues of which the Northern League was one and as I was refereeing in that particular competition at the time I felt that perhaps at the end of the first season under the new set-up I might be given the chance to get on the Football League line.

But before I had quite recovered from what I considered to be long term encouragement I received an even bigger surprise. The Football League invited half a dozen onto their list immediately and I was one . . . admitted before the new system had a chance to work.

I was fortunate enough to spend only one season on the line before I was accepted as a Football League referee. Looking back 1966 was an exceptional year for English football. We won the World Cup, of course, and without sounding too big-headed I feel that the new intake of referees that year was particularly impressive. Gordon Hill, Roger Kirkpatrick, Iorwerth Jones, Gordon Kew, John Homewood and Clive Thomas all joined the League ranks at the same time as myself. I doubt if any other year has yielded quite such a crop.

I have often been asked if I consider a referee's apprenticeship laborious or even unnecessary. The answer is 'no.' There is no short cut to the top and frankly I do not believe there should be. It took me 13 years to reach League status and I needed every one of those years to gain all the qualities a top whistler requires. Sure, I felt frustrated at times as all young men in all walks of life feel frustrated. The impatience of youth is well known. But thankfully authority forced me to ride out the frustrations.

A typical example was when, in the full flush of becoming a Class One ref, I applied for acceptance to the Northern Intermediate League. My theory was that a young referee for a young league was ideal. I applied when I was 24, again when I was 25, and yet again when I was 26 but on each occasion received no joy. I was bitter and wondered who had the knife in for me but that was stupid, of course.

The Durham FA were merely showing more wisdom in not recommending me to the NIL than I had at the time and for that I am grateful.

No, I have no axe to grind. The system made me what I am today.

3 Explosive Start

The Football League received me as a lion rather than a lamb. That is not to say I felt like some beast prepared to devour all in its way. More that my introduction was, shall we say, full-blooded.

Take my first ever Division One match as a referee for example. I was nicknamed Penalty Partridge by the newspapers (what a Godsend I've been to the media with my surname) and clashed strongly with one of England's new World Cup heroes Gordon Banks into the bargain.

The match was in March, 1967 between Manchester City and Leicester City at Maine Road and the banner headlines 'Penalty Partridge' came about because I had the temerity to award no fewer than three spot kicks during the game. The confrontation with Banks – my first but certainly not my last – was because I dared to award the first against his team.

I have always found Gordon Banks to be a player who believed in his own publicity. There are certain footballers who think that because they are big stars they have rights not available to others. They are above the law to some degree. Banks was one of those players. I have never accepted such arguments and consequently Gordon and I have had our moments.

A wonderful goalkeeper, he was nevertheless excitable under pressure and he lost his head at Maine Road when Glyn Pardoe, who had seen his first attempted cross blocked by Bobby Roberts, tried again and Richie Norman handled.

There was no question in my mind that it was a spot kick but Banks chased me round the penalty area like someone demented. When I placed the ball on the 12-yard spot it was kicked away. The fuss was awful and Banks was a lucky man. If he had acted so irresponsibly two years later I would have cautioned him but here was England's World Cup winning goalkeeper pressurising a referee in his first Division One match and my inexperience showed inasmuch as I awarded the penalty but did not administer the caution.

Johnny Crossan rifled the kick home low to Banks' left but the laugh was that after all the commotion Leicester went on to win 3–1 and smash Manchester City's unbeaten run of 11 games. Winger Jackie Sinclair scored twice from the spot after being fouled himself by Bobby Kennedy and then Crossan tripping Paul Matthews.

Mike Stringfellow completed the scoring – from a free-kick.

Only weeks after that Gordon Banks signed for Stoke City and I reported him to the Football League for being improperly dressed in a match at West Bromwich. He turned out in a jersey he had been asked to sponsor with a black collar, piping on the sleeves and buttons at the neck which, of course, could have been extremely dangerous had they come off during play. We had only just received a letter from the League reminding us of the mode of dress for players and consequently I told Banks to change at half-time.

The report to the League was a necessary safeguard. If some eagle-eyed reporter had spotted the change and then asked Banks about it without consulting me and Alan Hardaker had read the resulting story I would have been for the high jump.

For those who think such a thing trivial let me give an example of the Football League's attitude to such changes.

I have always felt it wise to inform Lytham of such decisions I made, however small, rather than run the risk of them finding out through a third party and such devotion to duty got me a smart reprimand early in my career.

I wrote to headquarters:

Dear Sir,

Bury v Mansfield Town.

In the above game played at Bury on Saturday 10th February 1968 I was requested by the trainer of Mansfield Town about 30 minutes before kick-off to check the colour of their shorts against the colour of the Bury shorts.

I am aware of the League regulation which states that only shirts and stockings can be changed should there be a clash in colours; nevertheless in this instance, when the shorts of both clubs were an identical colour of blue, I suggested to Mansfield that if they had white shorts they could change and avoid any clash of colour whatsoever.

Mansfield played in white shorts and Bury played in blue shorts.

> Yours faithfully,
> Pat Partridge.
> Referee

Back came the reply.

Dear Sir,

Bury v Mansfield Town.

I have to acknowledge receipt of your letter of the 15th instant.

If the two clubs played in the colours registered in the Handbook, then you were entirely wrong in acceding to the request of the Mansfield Trainer.

These people are beginning to make trouble where trouble does not exist, and if you were aware – as you say – of the provisions of the Football League regulation in this matter, then I think it would have been more appropriate for you to have pointed out to the Mansfield Trainer regarding the regulation, and refused his request.

Yours faithfully

A. Hardaker.

Secretary.

My biggest dispute with Gordon Banks came during the 1971 FA Cup semi-final when his club, Stoke City, were deprived of a Wembley appearance by an Arsenal equaliser from the penalty spot in injury time. Stoke lost the replay and Arsenal went on to do the League and Cup double.

Banksy claimed afterwards that he was pushed in the back when a Geordie Armstrong free-kick was flighted into the box with Stoke leading 2–1 but that I awarded a corner instead of a foul. From Armstrong's corner kick Frank McLintock bulleted a header which, with Banks beaten, John Mahoney handled on the line and Peter Storey equalised from the penalty.

The flashpoint was the moment Armstrong's free-kick dropped in the Stoke box and not the penalty decision. Tony Waddington naturally took up the cry after the game and said something to the effect that if Gordon Banks said it was a foul then it was a foul because he was that sort of person. He wouldn't lie. I wondered if the implication was that I would.

It was a set piece incident and I was bang up with play. In my opinion, and my eyes are as good as the next man's, it was a corner. If it were not I have one question to ask: Why did Gordon Banks and Stoke City wait until after the game when the corner had produced a penalty to squeal?

Banksy and his defenders never attempted to swallow me when they thought they could easily clear the corner kick and then the final whistle would go.

No, I find that managers and players of unsuccessful teams often come up with excuses in the after-match inquests which were never raised at the time of the alleged offence. Banksy nailed me and so did Tony Waddington but I prefer the honesty of John Mahoney. He said: 'What could I do? I wanted to head the ball away and I tried to make it look as though I'd headed it but it was no good.' He had tried it on but when the con failed he was man enough to admit it.

If my first Division One game brought me notoriety as Penalty Partridge then my third in the top flight was another to hit the headlines.

It was Manchester United's First Division championship party held at Old Trafford on May 13, 1967 when Stoke City were the visitors and 63,000 people turned up to salute their heroes. The preliminaries were emotional in the extreme with David Herd plodding stoically to the middle on crutches to receive his championship medal and Matt Busby purring his gratitude to the fans.

The match itself never lived up to its billing perhaps because nothing was at stake. There was the odd flash of genius from George Best wearing Denis Law's No 8 shirt, no goals, and what was described by one writer as 'the ugliest clash Old Trafford has seen for many a match.'

That flare-up was to have far reaching effects witnessed as it was by millions of TV viewers who flooded the Football League with complaints and it eventually led to a change in the laws of the game. Yet the most offending part of the whole incident I never even saw. It happened like this: Paddy Crerand and Peter Dobing suddenly lost their heads and had a real go at each other. Fortunately I was right on the spot and I jumped in smartly to drag them apart. Players were jostling for position and I had my arm round Crerand restraining him so that his face was directly over my right shoulder close in. Unknown to me while he was actually leaning over my shoulder he spat at one of the Stoke players, left-half Tony Allen. Naturally I couldn't see it – it happened out of my line of vision but the angle of the TV camera was such that Crerand was in full view.

When everyone quietened down I cautioned Crerand and Dobing for the original incident and restarted the game. No one mentioned the spitting either then or after the game. I drove home blissfully happy and unaware of the pandemonium which was to be released that night on Match of the Day.

We only had an old black and white telly at the time so Margaret and I popped round to my parents to watch the game. When I saw Crerand's face loom up on the screen I could have been sick. I thought : 'My God, he's been allowed to get away with it.'

Luckily from my point of view all the League's top brass such as president Len Shipman and secretary Alan Hardaker had been at the game to see Manchester United receive their championship trophy and therefore they knew at first hand what had happened but the inevitable letter came eleven days later.

Dear Mr Partridge,

Manchester United v Stoke City.

The Football League are receiving numerous complaints regarding an incident in the above Match, which was very clearly shown on Television, involving P. Crerand of Manchester United and a Stoke City player.

I have received the note of your caution to P. Crerand but

I would like to have your observations regarding the other incident.

> Yours Sincerely,
> A Hardaker.
> Secretary.

I wrote back stating that, in fact, I had seen nothing of the 'other incident' because of the position of myself and Crerand at that moment. Though Crerand was dragged before a disciplinary committee which sat at the Midland Hotel in Derby the following August to consider the spitting charge I was not called to give evidence. The minutes of the meeting contain the paragraph :

'The Committee, limited in the action it could take by the Rules of the Football Association, ordered Crerand to give a written undertaking to the Football Association within seven days not to repeat such action in the future and further warned him that if he did so he would be suspended.'

As a direct result of the Paddy Crerand affair pressure was brought to bear on the FA and Football League and the following year the International Board changed the law to make spitting an offence punishable by dismissal from the field of play.

Had I actually witnessed Crerand's action I would have ordered him off in that game. He was being cautioned for ungentlemanly conduct and a second caution for spitting would have meant automatic dismissal. What surprised me about it all was the action, or lack of it, by Tony Allen. He showed immense restraint in the face of provocation. How he didn't hit Crerand I'll never know. I am certain that under similar circumstances I would have snapped. I would admire a player more who cracked another on the whiskers and walked off than one who spit at him. At least the first is manly. The second, in my opinion, is the lowest of the low.

I must say, however, that I have never had any trouble with Paddy Crerand since. Nor has either of us held a grudge. I met him many times when he was still playing and later when he was in management and he always had a cheery 'hello' and a smile.

If there is a major influence on every career, something which happened relatively early on and set a standard by which others came to judge you, then for me it occurred when I penalised Tommy Docherty's Aston Villa for blatant time wasting. The lasting effect, I believe, was to give all footballers an idea of my attitude to the game. In short I earned their respect as a bloke who couldn't be messed around.

The match was in the 1968–69 season at Preston when Villa, who had committed the same sin against Carlisle in a previous game started their old tactics.

I took aside the team's captain Brian Tiler and told him: 'Look, I haven't got a train to catch. I'm prepared to stay until midnight if necessary to get this game finished.' I approached their goalkeeper, John Dunn, and dished out the same message.

Villa took no heed and I added a full five minutes onto the game. The inevitable happened, of course – Preston scrambled a winner through their skipper and full-back Jim McNab in the dying seconds.

The Doc went bananas, flinging about soccer's most over-worked word 'diabolical' like confetti. I was a wrong 'un, a bandit. In the heat of his first defeat as Villa boss he agreed that his side had wasted time at Carlisle but not at Preston. Now there's a thing.

Me? I must speak as I find and I like the Doc. He blows hot and cold and he has got himself into some terrible

scrapes but he's up front. By that I mean he tells you to
your face, then forgets it. Give me that type to the sly,
knife-in-the-back sort any time.

There was no thought of being controversial or clever at
Deepdale. Only that football is supposed to be a game of
90 minutes duration and that 90 minutes would be PLAYED.
The week before I had added on time when Bradford were
winning and time wasting and they went and scored again.
There was neither shouting nor headlines then but I
suppose poor Bradford hardly had the charisma of Tommy
Doc. Or the lungs!

The Press lads gave it all a right old airing and the papers
carried letter after letter from supporters all applauding
my efforts to promote football and not negative tactics. Roy
Ullyett even produced a cartoon in the Daily Express showing a ref standing over the Doc as the sun comes up over
the ground saying: 'Mr Docherty, I don't care if it is Sunday
morning and you're due to sing in the choir – the game goes
on.'

The upshot of it all was that I won an award. Or shared
one with . . . the Doc.

We were voted Sports Personalities of the Month by the
London Sportsman Club – me for what one of the judges
described as 'doing more for football in 95 minutes at
Preston than the Football Associations of the world have
done in the last 95 months.' Tommy's award was for his
achievements as Villa manager.

Unfortunately our re-union in London when Denis Compton was to hand over the prizes never took place. I had a
previous refereeing engagement that night. No doubt the
Doc thought I was wasting time.

4   Players . . .

Whoever first said football is all about players must have been a real deep thinker. They are obviously the men who matter and I've had a lot closer look than most at all the big stars of the last decade or more.

It has been a privilege to share the field with some. A nightmare with others. But they are, good or bad, talented or otherwise, the very heart of this great game.

In the next few pages I would like to relive some moments of fun, some of drama, and draw a few conclusions about the stars.

And fun almost inevitably involved Nobby Stiles, the little fella with the toothless grin and funny walk who endeared himself to everyone when England won the World Cup at Wembley. Stiles had a sense of humour, right enough, but he was a hard man into the bargain and the combination of the two showed itself during a floodlit League game between Manchester United and Burnley at Old Trafford.

Burnley's centre-forward Andy Lochhead was giving Nobby the runaround. Nobby kept snapping at Andy's heels and in the first-half I whispered to him to cut it out. Nobby apologised then grinned. And so it went on, Lochhead buzzing about and Nobby a little terrier at his feet. Then, in the second-half, Nobby caught him and I said: 'Okay, next time you're cautioned.' Sure enough, there was a next time.

Andy was streaking towards goal when Nobby clipped him from behind.

Out came my book and Stiles, full of apologies, pleaded: 'It's the floodlights, ref. They shine in my contact lenses and I can't see a thing.' As I was writing Nobby leaned over and said: 'You spell it with an "I" not a "Y." ' And he was supposed to have bad eyesight.

It is that sort of repartee which I love between player and referee. It is healthy and full of mutual respect. Nobby knew he had to be cautioned and he accepted it. There was no animosity between us and if you could get on to that level in other situations half of football's problems would be solved.

Nobby and Tommy Smith are the sort I would always have in my team. Smith would play for 90 minutes and then if Shanks had asked him to run through a brick wall he would have done it. Football is a man's game and I like it to be played by men.

I remember Smithy getting an elbow in the face once as he went to head the ball. He was out cold and we all gathered round. 'Where am I?' he moaned. 'Who did it? I'll effing get 'im.'

'No, Tommy,' I said. 'Forget it. He's not as hard as you.'

Stiles, Smith and Norman Hunter are all the same. You must be around when they put their visiting card in, put in yours, and say: 'Right, who is next?' Hunter and Everton's Colin Harvey clashed so hard one day, fair but like two runaway steamrollers with no quarter given, that I stopped the game to ask if they were both all right and then restarted it with a dropped ball. No foul had been committed.

I admire skill as well as courage, of course, and in that first category I must put Bobby Charlton an elegant player who glides rather than runs. But I must qualify any praise of Charlton by adding that he is one of the biggest moaners I have ever come across on the field. He even bitched unmercifully last year, long after his first-class career was over, when I reffed a testimonial match at York in which he was playing. He appealed for a foul throw and to be truthful he was right but I let it go because it was in no-man's land and it was only a benefit match. The flow of the game seemed to be more important to entertain the crowd. But the other team broke away with Charlton still moaning and scored a goal. He was livid.

I first got his number during the days when he was a vital cog in a magnificently adventurous Manchester United team. I have a habit of calling the captain 'Skip' if we are not on first name terms and during the course of a game I said: 'By the way, Skip ...' I never got any further. 'Don't call me Skip,' snapped Charlton. 'It sounds like something out of a comic book.'

Using Christian names of players generally breaks down any barriers though it is viewed on the odd occasion with suspicion.

During a Norwich–Tottenham game a few years ago Martin Peters – then playing for Spurs – made a bad pass and I quipped: 'Come on Martin, you can do better than that.' Doug Livermore heard me and shouted: 'What's all this then, ref – is he a personal friend of yours or something?' Luckily I knew Livermore's first name and replied: 'Okay Doug, what's your problem then?' It killed off any thoughts of favouritism and Livermore was happy.

Jack Charlton is a different type of man to his brother Bobby. More of an extrovert, less of a stylist he was difficult to handle as a player only because of his clumsy gait and clenched teeth determination. He caused hell, and became famous, for standing on the opposing goal-line in front of the goalkeeper for corner kicks. All elbows and giraffe neck he was. Defenders used to go mad claiming he deliberately impeded the keeper but I thought it was a tremendous tactic. He was the complete decoy moving briskly away as the ball swung over with panic stricken opponents too late to pick him up. I never once had to penalise him for pushing the keeper.

Bob Wilson often used to moan about Big Jack whose stock answer was 'Aye, I push him all right – usually with both his hands in my back.'

Jack became a good friend during his time as manager of Middlesbrough and I admired his single mindedness. He said when he arrived that he would only stay four years believing that familiarity can breed contempt among players and he walked out the Ayresome door four years to the day though the directors begged him to stay. When he won promotion to the First Division by the length of the Tees he refused to milk the adulation as so many managers do. Instead he pointed out that the team had been assembled by the previous manager Stan Anderson and gave him a public 'thank you.' A big, big man in more ways than one.

Two of Charlton's old team-mates at Leeds deserve a special mention – the little fellas in the engine-room Johnny Giles and Billy Bremner.

Giles is the finest passer of a ball I have ever come across. I used to marvel at him. He enthralled me. Once against Burnley he was really excelling himself. The wind was bad, swirling in sudden gusts, and the surface was bumpy but Giles was stroking the ball about with great arrogant authority. One pass through the eye of a needle to Eddie Gray was so superb that as I ran past I said: 'Do you play snooker, Johnny?' He was so accurate that it was like using a billiard cue. He made passing a simple exercise.

The most frequent accusation against Bremner was that he tried to referee matches. That was rubbish at least when I was around. Sure, he yapped away all the time and he challenged decisions you made but never in a way which you could send him off. It was all down to respect – if he had that for you it was all right.

I remember driving away from Anfield after a Liverpool–Leeds match, which were always highly competitive with both teams superbly talented and as hard as nails, and Alan Hardaker was speaking on Sports Report on the radio. 'At least we had a referee today who treated men like men and let them get on with the game,' he said. That was what Billy Bremner liked.

With that mop of curly red hair and fiery temper he was the player the fans loved to hate but I'll tell you something . . . those same fans would have loved their club to have bought him.

George Best, like Bremner, attracted trouble which was not always of his own making and therefore demanded protection from the man in the middle.

Players would bait him hoping for a response which would see him ordered off. They knew he had a short fuse and was an easy target for that sort of treatment. He blew hot and cold very quickly and the answer was to try and get in close whenever he was involved because he could snap.

I'll give you an example. Manchester United were playing Huddersfield at Old Trafford and Besty, who had scored United's goal, was having his shirt stretched out of his shorts by Jimmy Lawson. He spun round angrily on the Huddersfield winger and arms were raised. Best pushed off Lawson then reeled back holding his face. I dived in between them and said: 'Don't be two silly little devils. Get on with the game and enjoy it.' I didn't caution either of them.

The amount of natural God-given ability George Best had was unbelievable. At his peak I put him in the same class as Beckenbauer, Pele and Cruyff. No one can say more than that.

Denis Law was a fascinating player, a great player. Razor sharp reflexes and a nose for goals which really did make him the king. His sort of talent is rare and I believe he knows it. I met him at the TV Colour Centre in Buenos Aires during the World Cup after he had come down from the disaster area of Cordoba and we got talking about the Coca Cola kids. Remember them – they were the lads who juggled with a ball keeping it up on their feet, arms, knees and head a hundred times or more. I ventured that it might be a good idea in this country as half-time entertainment to keep the crowd happy. 'Our pro's wouldn't allow it,' sniffed Law. 'It would show the buggers up.'

He was no angel was our Denis but he still supported me after the 1978 League Cup final replay when TV did a crucifying job on me over the penalty which won Nottingham Forest the trophy. I was back at Old Trafford the following week and Denis was having a cup of tea. 'That was a disgrace,' he said. 'Carving up a ref like that on telly shouldn't be allowed. It does the game a tremendous amount of harm.' To be truthful I was taken aback by Law's attitude. I felt he might have been pleased to see a leading referee pilloried. 'It's about time,' was the comment I would have expected but here was a bloke who could hardly be described as a referee's best friend realising the fact that trial by television is a dangerous growth in football.

The line taken by another ex-striker, Derek Dougan, over the same incident was much more predictable. He criticised me in no uncertain terms presumably feeling that he had a better view of play from his seat in the stand than I had from only a few yards away. Fair enough, the man is entitled to his opinion.

But there is another thing involving myself about which he made a big song and dance which is not a matter of opinion. It is fact – and the Doog got it wrong.

I cautioned Dougan during Wolves' FA Cup semi-final against Leeds at Maine Road in April, 1973 for a second-half charge on goalkeeper David Harvey and after the game Derek began mouthing to all the Press. He was widely quoted as saying: 'I made what I thought was a perfectly fair challenge against Harvey. I couldn't believe it when the referee pulled me up. It is the first time I have been booked for charging a goalkeeper in 15 years as a player.'

Wrong. Just over five years previously – on Saturday October 14, 1967 to be precise – I had cautioned Dougan for an elbows-and-knees challenge on Manchester City keeper Ken Mulhearn at Maine Road. The same referee on the same ground for the same offence . . . and if Derek Dougan still doesn't believe it he is more than welcome to come to my house and take a look at the proof in my scrapbook.

That is the perfect example of players who open their mouths and think afterwards. I don't like untruths but certain footballers deal in them without the decency to even blush.

The Doog is a real Walter Mitty character. He believes he can put the world to right, he's an amateur politician with the happy knack of promoting himself.

I was disappointed in him during his time as chairman of the Professional Footballers' Association. A lot was achieved of which he must take his share of credit but his attitude was not always what it might have been. I'm thinking, for example, of when the Committee of Study was set up at Lancaster Gate to try and bring some sanity back into the game.

A cross section of football was represented. Lord West-wood, Alan Hardaker and George Readle from the Football League; Dougan, Cliff Lloyd and Bruce Bannister from the PFA; Ron Greenwood, Don Revie, Alan Dicks and Bill McGarry from the Secretaries and Managers Association; and myself, Gordon Kew, Dick Hall and Vince James from the Association of Football League Referees and Linesmen. Dr Andrew Stephen was in the chair and FA secretary Ted Croker was also present.

I was president of our association and I made an impassioned plea for referees and players to get together more to produce a better understanding. The immediate reaction of Hardaker was: 'Tremendous. Any time you want an office for a meeting there's one at Lytham for you.' Croker, too, offered to house us. But Dougan was not in raptures and there was nothing forthcoming from him afterwards. Without the backing of the most important body of people there was no hope, of course.

Cliff Lloyd I've always had a lot of time for and I am delighted that Gordon Taylor is Dougan's successor as chairman. He is a sensible lad and is no trouble at all on the park.

Taylor is one of the new breed of deep thinking players who care not just about themselves but the state of the game generally. That is not to say others are totally self centred only less inclined to realise that football stretches beyond 90 minutes on a Saturday.

Players like Alan Gowling, Steve Heighway, Steve Coppell and Brian Hall you can talk to and reason with. Others like Peter Osgood and Peter Storey, who used to be with Arsenal, you cannot.

I had no time for Osgood or Storey full stop. They were surly players who did their profession no good as far as I was concerned and I would never attempt to get into a conversation with either during a match. Ossie felt superior and would often stand, hands on hips, trying to belittle those around him be they other players or the referee.

He was blessed with talent all right but I felt he never used it to the full. The sort of relationship I prefer to remember was shown by Gordon McQueen when Manchester United entertained Everton a couple of seasons back.

Bob Latchford and Terry Darracott went for the same ball in the United penalty area and there was a clash of heads. It seemed nothing at the time. Indeed the crowd thought it was hilarious but then McQueen said : 'Quick ref, stop the game.' I went over and there was blood pouring all over the place. Here was a situation where McQueen could have ignored what had happened. Both the players hurt were in the opposing team and Gordon's not known as the softest player in the world, is he? But at that moment he forgot all about hard professionalism and was genuinely concerned for two fellow pros. I can still see Everton's manager Gordon Lee making a point of shaking McQueen's hand at the end of the game.

McQueen is fearless in his approach to the game and so was another centre-half from the old days Bob McKinlay who made a record 611 first team appearances for Nottingham Forest. At Burnley I literally picked his teeth from the squelching mud of the penalty area after they had been kicked out by a flying boot. A cheap and painful way of having an extraction.

I have long felt that the football writers would do the game a great service if occasionally they voted Player of the Year someone who was not in the League championship side or appearing at Wembley in the Cup final two days after the presentation. Preferably a player who is not a household name and therefore feted time and time again. My own nominations in the past would have included McKinlay, Rowdy Yeats (Liverpool), John Barnwell (Arsenal and Nottingham Forest) and Chris Balderstone (Carlisle). They were true gentlemen.

Finally a funny story . . . we were at Stoke for a night game when the Victoria Ground was no more than a mudheap and a Stoke player, I think it was John Marsh, went to clear a ball. 'I've lost it, I've flippin' lost it,' he yelled running round in circles like a demented ostrich. 'Lost what?' I asked him fearing the worst. 'My contact lense, that's what. It's fallen out,' he said.

Obviously it was impossible to stop the game so I quickly dropped a two bob bit in the area concerned and carried on. At the end I hunted out the groundsman and told him: 'There's two bob out there on the pitch and when you find it there's a contact lense near as well.' I was still in the bath when there was a knock on the door. It was the groundsman looking as though he had just won the pools. 'Here's your money,' he said flicking the coin across to me. 'Oh, and we found the contact lense as well. It was only a couple of feet away.'

5 Managers...

Managers basically fall into two categories – the face to face let's-get-it-sorted type and the read-what-I-think-in-the-newspapers type. Needless to say I much prefer the first.

Football is all about opinion, certain decisions I make in all honesty during the course of a game can be open to interpretation, and therefore I not only fully expect those who may suffer to disagree but for them to voice it as well. However I expect it to be man to man in private. If general quotes appear later then perhaps it is regrettable but it is still acceptable.

What I take exception to are the managers who say not a word, either deliberately avoiding me or giving a watery smile, then throw around the most torrid of accusations in the Press.

Malcolm Allison, who is now back at Manchester City, is a colourful character with whom I have had a few, shall we say, confrontations strictly of the first nature. A big man who loves the limelight, he will flaunt himself before a crowd in a huge fedora hat blue smoke billowing from the biggest cigar imaginable. Champagne is his idea of drinking water.

His tongue is often overworked and constantly in danger of getting him onto the wrong side of officialdom but despite our set-to's I believe he is good for the game. I like the man immensely.

Maine Road is a ground which for some strange reason has left me feeling uneasy on occasions. It has nothing to do with the club or the supporters. They are fine. It is merely an inexplicable thing which footballers will fully understand.

One day I was walking off at half-time with my linesmen and I spotted Big Mal down the tunnel standing by the City dressing-room. He was seething and I steeled myself for a verbal battle. Suddenly a hand shot out, grabbed him, and he disappeared into the dressing-room. My relief was immense but the reprieve was to be a short one.

As we emerged for the second-half I could see Allison's huge frame menacingly near the mouth of the tunnel. 'This is it,' I thought and I told my linesmen to go on I would be out in a moment. Privacy with no witnesses to inhibit the conversation or make trouble afterwards seemed infinitely the best idea. I walked straight up to Allison and said: 'What's on your mind, then?'

'You're having a bloody nightmare,' he exploded.

'Look,' I said. 'You know that, I know that and there are 30,000 people out there who know that. Now what about you. Do you want sending to Coventry?'

I was referring to the fact that Allison was lined up for the Coventry manager's post (chairman Derek Robins had actually offered him it) but Mal in his usual style had been unable to stay quiet and had broke the story in the previous morning's papers . . . a fact which was to cost him the job.

He looked stunned for a moment then said: 'Touche, ref!' and stalked off down the corridor.

On another occasion Allison suggested I had been intimidated by the crowd during a cup-tie at Liverpool. 'When you come to Anfield you get fouls against you that are not fouls. It's well known in football,' boomed Malcolm.

The figures were thirty-seven free-kicks against City and

fourteen against Liverpool with one player on each side cautioned. Allison had stoked up the game all week in the papers and City had played it hard but it was niggly rather than dirty.

Big Mal, knowing there was a replay to come, was draining every drop out of the drama but he wasn't supported by his own players in his opinion of my performance. Franny Lee went into print telling his manager to shut up and added: 'I thought Partridge did a good job. He kept a firm grip and if he hadn't this game could have ended in a brawl but it was never remotely like that.' Skipper Tony Book, cautioned for a foul on Steve Heighway, added: 'The ref did a good job. I was late with my tackle.'

Anyway, City won the replay 2–0 and Allison was all sweetness and light. That's him – he can say things and sometimes get away with things you would strongly object to from other managers because there is so much honest emotion which bubbles over yet so much genuine friendship under the surface. There's no undercurrent of malice which sometimes prevails in others.

Allison's former partner at Maine Road, Joe Mercer, is someone I hold in not quite the same affection. To the public he's genial Joe of the craggy face and whimsical smile. A character in short. That's as may be but our relationship is based round an incident in the Anfield guest lounge which left me extremely angry.

Mercer was then manager of Coventry City who had lost by the odd goal and he was holding forth with a group of friends only a few yards from where my wife was having a quiet cup of tea waiting for me to get ready.

Margaret's used to overhearing uncomplimentary things uttered mainly in the heat of a defeat which demands an excuse. Human nature being what it is she has come to accept the inevitability of such happenings and, by and large, she is unflustered. Mercer, however, was a bit strong and when his wife pointed out rather sheepishly that the referee's wife was in earshot he turned round, looked deliberately at Margaret, and said in a loud voice: 'I don't care if it is his wife. That was a diabolical decision.'

The need for a man of Joe Mercer's stature to turn on a woman in public and chide her for something her husband was supposed to have done was something I couldn't forgive. My wife was on her own; Mercer was bolstered by the support of friends. It seemed an uneven and unnecessary contest. I was the one who should have been on the end of any comments. It was only in the car on the way home that I heard what had happened and I was furious. Much more furious than Margaret, in fact, who thought Mercer's comments were childish. I don't see why she should ever suffer for me – a ref can be blasted as fair game but never his family.

There was a sequel a few weeks later when a Coventry player whom I had cautioned in that Liverpool game asked for a personal hearing which was held in Manchester. Mercer appealed on behalf of the player and, as is usual at these things, began cross examining me over the events leading up to the caution. I was aggressive with my answers and wouldn't elaborate – I couldn't honestly help it. The caution was duly recorded by the FA disciplinary committee and as Mercer left the hearing he mumbled: 'We can't beat this bugger on the field and we can't beat him here either.'

Bob Lord, chairman of the commission, asked me to stay behind and took me up on my aggressive attitude towards Mercer. Dickie Bird was equally perturbed. 'It isn't like you, Pat. What's wrong?' he said. He was right – it's never been my style to show anything but the courtesy such an occasion demands. I had let Joe Mercer get under my skin to such an extent that others could see it which wasn't good.

'I'm sorry,' I said, 'but it's personal with this fellow. I prefer not to go into it if you don't mind.' My apology was accepted with some scratching of the head.

To be fair it must be added that Joe Mercer got up at the Secretaries and Managers Association dinner after my FA Cup final of '75 and spoke in glowing terms of my handling of the game. He could have avoided mention of it altogether after our previous brushes.

The way to accept defeat, unlike Mercer's at Anfield, is best illustrated by Steve Burtenshaw. After his team, Queen's Park Rangers, lost 2–1 to Derby County at the Baseball Ground last season in a match where they desperately needed the points to pull away from a relegation position Burtenshaw wrote to me as follows:

Dear Pat,

Just a quick line to say how sorry I was to miss you after the game last Saturday because I wanted to thank you and say how impressed I was with your refereeing display.

I have no wish to talk out of turn Pat but if a few of your colleagues would appreciate as well as you obviously do the frustration that some players feel during a game and not take some of their comments personally, then I am sure that the mutual respect between players and officials that appears to be lessening at the moment, will return very quickly. Please don't get me wrong when I say that in my view the best referees appear to develop a thicker skin and this fact is very much appreciated by both players and management of the professional clubs. It certainly does not mean that any game is less controllable as you proved so admirably last weekend.

Believe it or not Pat, I am not in the habit of writing such letters as this but as I have all too often seen my players booked for far less than occurred last Saturday, it gives me pleasure and assurance when referees do not always take the easy way out but handle the situation without the necessity of booking players and still keep control of the game.

> Best wishes
> Your sincerely,
> Steve Burtenshaw.

The passing reference by Burtenshaw to missing me after the game may be a small point but such courtesies are what this game is built upon. Bill Shankly always went out of his way to seek me out for a chat during his time at Liverpool. Win, lose or draw Shanks would pop in to pass the time of day and on the only occasion I escaped (I think he was called away for a television interview or something) he actually phoned my house twice the next day to make up for it. What made him stand apart from the average was that he recognised referees and linesmen as an integral part of the game and his attitude was greatly appreciated by us all.

A first-rate man with boundless enthusiasm, he talked with the rapidity of a machine gun. Yet his words were gems not so much hot air. I have never known him publicly attack a referee. It was almost as though it were below his dignity.

A much more complex character is the man who last year lifted the First Division championship for the second time with two different clubs each built from the depths of Division Two. That alone makes him extra special among managers. I refer to Brian Clough, creator of modern-day Derby County and Nottingham Forest.

Clough is a mass of contradictions. A brusque person one moment capable of the most hurtful of actions, a kind and thoughtful companion the next.

How do you fathom a man who forgot as a matter of courtesy to even say thank you to the three officials who handled his testimonial match at Sunderland yet will pay the butcher's bill of an old lady who, having had her order weighed, finds she cannot afford it? Brian Clough did both those things.

He also won the hearts of an entire county Durham primary school by arriving unannounced at their open day shortly after Forest had won the League championship. The headmaster George Green, a former League linesman, had asked Clough if he would attend and he said yes . . . providing there was no publicity. George also approached me without letting on about the other guest, and when I got there and Brian Clough drove through the gates you could have knocked me down with a feather. He had the kids spellbound and to this day they talk of the great man. Hardly the actions of a so-called headline-hogger, was it?

Much more in character with his public image was the time last season I had to postpone a match at the City Ground because of snow. Clough knew a quick way back onto the motorway and suggested I followed him. He swung his huge Merc across the main road, stuck his hand out of the window to bring the busy rush-hour traffic screeching to a halt, and waved me out. That's the same fellow who, while at Brighton, went out for a walk and got knocked down by a speedboat!

Beating Brian Clough at his own game is a rarity – but I've done it. During the days when referees went into the dressing-rooms prior to a game I took Derby County in a League Cup second round match with Halifax Town. As we were getting ready I turned to my two linesmen and said: 'I'll tell you what'll happen when we go in to see Derby. All the players will be sitting ready and Clough will be relaxing full length on the treatment table. There'll be complete silence. When I'm finished talking I'll ask "Any questions?" and no one will say a word. But just as I get to the door Cloughie will say something.'

In we went. Every player was stripped, sitting fidgeting. Clough was full length. I launched into my spiel and finished up asking the players: 'Any questions?' Not a word was uttered. I turned to leave and as my hand reached the door knob the silence was punctuated by those famous nasal tones. 'By the way, referee . . .' Before the sentence could be completed I snapped over my shoulder: 'I wasn't talking to you. I was talking to the players' and shut the door with a bang. I could almost see Clough's open mouth from the corridor.

The linesmen thought it hilarious but they refused to believe that I hadn't actually rehearsed the whole thing with Clough.

He's gone on record as saying: 'Mr Partridge isn't one of my favourite referees' though his timing was ironical as it turned out. It was just before last year's League Cup final when Forest won as a direct result of a penalty award which was considered more than a trifle controversial.

Gordon Lee has been much kinder in his public utterances about me right from his early days as boss of Port Vale. As long ago as February 1973 he tipped me for the top after his side had been slaughtered 5–0 at Brentford. And in recent times in a strong attack on the retirement age of forty-seven for referees Gordon said: 'If anybody asks me to think about a referee I immediately think of Pat Partridge who is great, knows what football is all about, and does the job very well. The point is that Pat is far better now than when he first came into the game and to me it is a great tragedy that when referees have accumulated all the knowledge and knowhow built up over the years that somehow at forty-seven they can no longer play any part in the game. To me I liken the referee to a surgeon. Do you want a young chap of twenty-five full of enthusiasm but lacking in experience or do you prefer somebody aged, say forty-five or forty-seven, experienced over the years with full knowledge of technique? The choice is obvious.'

While I take such words from a top manager as a tremendous compliment and rather like the analogy of the surgeon I'm afraid I must disagree with him on the retirement age. At this precise time with less than a season to go before I am forced to step down perhaps I should be advocating radical changes but in truth I cannot. FIFA's age limit is fifty to our forty-seven and an extra three years would obviously be more than welcome from my point of view. However there has to be a ceiling somewhere and I knew when I entered the profession precisely what it was. Had I not accepted it I shouldn't have joined.

If I go back some way with Gordon Lee then Lawrie McMenemy and I have an even longer association. We grew up together in the amateur Northern League when I was making my way in the world of refereeing and Lawrie was manager of Bishop Auckland. Early March, 1967 saw me given the unusual distinction of handling my second Northern League Cup final. Tow Law v Bishops it was, only a fortnight after the pair had declared open warfare in a game which had inevitably seen the poor ref blasted. Folk were expecting similar trouble again with memories still fresh but it went off like a charm. Bishops won the cup and I don't think Lawrie ever forgot it. He's always told his players: 'This bloke will give you no favours so don't try anything on.'

McMenemy has a personality to match his size and after my FA Cup final appointment he quipped: 'Love all those photographs of you feeding the animals, Pat – I suppose it makes a change from booking 'em.'

I've mentioned Brian Clough's testimonial when he managed to avoid even shaking hands with his three match officials but Harold Shepherdson, Middlesbrough's assistant manager and England's 1966 World Cup trainer, was almost as bad. His thank you was a pair of cufflinks in a plastic case which were on sale in the Boro souvenir shop!

He didn't even hand them over personally. He thrust them into the hands of one of the linesmen, Lol Douglas, and asked him to dish them out.

Benefit games are not normally like that, of course. They are generally a joy because they are a way of paying tribute to a man's skill and I have been privileged to take the middle for countless players . . . Ian Porterfield, David Craig, John Hickton, Bobby Kerr, Jimmy Smith, Bill Gates and many, many more. I will never ever say 'no' if I can possibly help it.

It's not often that you get the opportunity to recruit someone from the opposite side of the fence but on one very, very famous occasion I had Jimmy Hill, the former Coventry City manager and well-known TV analyst, as my linesman in front of 45,000 people at Highbury. I would like to think that the experience has made him less critical of referees from his seat in the Match of the Day studios on a Saturday night.

The drama, which got massive TV and Press coverage, happened after only twelve minutes of Arsenal's First Division match with Liverpool. Linesman Dennis Drewitt turned quickly to follow play and his studs stuck in the turf wrenching his knee. It's an injury footballers often receive and Dennis had to be carried off on a stretcher.

A loudspeaker appeal brought forward three volunteers – a young Class Three referee, an ex-ref in his sixties, and Jimmy Hill from his seat in the Press box. The first was obviously too inexperienced and the second a little elderly for such a physical ordeal in front of a big crowd with the telly cameras present so Hill it was. He was an FA coach, knew the laws of the game, and I had no worries in pushing him on.

Before we restarted I brought both captains, Frank McLintock and Tommy Smith, together and told them: 'Look, this is not a gimmick. He'll do a good job if you give him a chance.' I also spoke with my other linesman demanding a little extra from him to take as much of the load off Hill as I could.

It would be the easiest thing in the world to knock his performance but in fact he did well under the circumstances. I got a flag when I needed one and in no way did he try to steal any thunder. The only shame was that the hold-up of almost quarter of an hour had caused the players to lose their rhythm and the game frizzled out into a goalless draw.

Perhaps the best insight into refereeing and lining comes from Jimmy Hill himself as a result of his seventy-eight minutes at Highbury and for that reason it's worth recording his feelings in some detail. This is what he said afterwards:

'I noticed that Arsenal's through runners, including both strikers and midfield players, make life more difficult for linesmen because of their constant dashes backward and forward deliberately aimed to avoid being caught offside. It's a positive aid in giving a correct offside decision to know what the forwards are trying to achieve.

'I also found the system of listening for the sound of the ball being kicked as it is played and looking for the forward's run, works perfectly. On one occasion it worked so well that the decision I made completely mystified the crowd, to say nothing of Alan Ball, but I knew I was right and I think the only man who would have agreed with me was Ray Kennedy, who had been caught offside for a fraction of a second, but that second happened to be the moment the ball was played through.

'Liverpool's forwards were different in style and were easier to spot in offside positions but Kevin Keegan particularly has to be watched carefully because he is always on the look-out to follow up a rebound from typically powerful long-range shots from Emlyn Hughes and Co.

'I was not called upon to make any decisions in relation to challenges and tackles, so carefully did Pat Partridge nurse me through the game, but throw-ins did prove difficult when the ball squirted into touch accidentally out of a tackle.'

Hill went on: 'It's pretty obvious that players seek to pressurise referees and linesmen to get their own way. Having been screeched at by fellow professionals in my playing days and done my share of screeching, too, I was hardly likely to be cowed.

'However, I appreciated on the day after the match what it must feel like for a linesman to have his performance pulled to pieces. It must be bad enough to have a decision challenged by someone with knowledge of the laws of the game, but to have to read the next day that you are at fault with a decision when you know you were right, must make linesmen feel like gunning down Press boxes and television studios.'

An attack on his integrity is the ultimate slur for a referee and sadly I suffered what I considered to be such an attack from Bob Stokoe when he was manager of Sunderland. He accused me, through the newspapers, of being biased against his team and costing them a cup-tie. The outburst, which included a swipe at the Football Association, was unforgivable and it was fifteen months before I spoke to the man again.

It all stemmed from my appointment to take the third

round tie between Carlisle United and Sunderland early in 1974 the season after Sunderland had won the FA Cup and the crux of the matter was geography. The proximity of my home to Roker Park.

What Stokoe did not know and what made some of his later accusations so wild was the background to my appointment. I arrived in England just before Christmas having spent ten weeks in Kuwait and popped in to see Reg Paine, the referees' secretary of the FA, at Lancaster Gate before travelling on home. He showed me the Cup draw and said : 'Look, if you have any objections you needn't handle the game. We've had no complaints from either Carlisle or Sunderland but it's up to you.' The reason for allocating me the tie was that the country was in the grip of a power crisis which meant no floodlit games plus petrol rationing and rail trouble and the FA were making certain that referees did not have to travel too far to matches. I said : 'Great, I'll do the game. I've never turned down an appointment yet and I'm not going to start now.'

When both managers came in with the team sheets at Brunton Park Stokoe began saying : 'We know it can be difficult for you,' but Alan Ashman cut him short. 'The man will do the job. Grow up, Bob, and leave it at that,' he said.

The game was a splendid one, goalless but chock full of good football. Carlisle wanted a penalty but it was a case of the ball hitting a player's hand rather than the other way round and the decision was accepted by the players without quibble. The Press went out of their way to mention my part and I vividly remember reading in the Sunday Express : 'Above all the game had superb refereeing from Pat Partridge. He booked Les O'Neill and Mickey Horswill in the second-half, was always right on the spot to control potentially explosive situations, and overall had the kind of match that stamps him as master of his craft.'

Four days later came the replay at Roker Park and Carlisle won 1–0. Once again it was a very good game, not difficult to handle, with a great atmosphere. Sunderland's players appealed for a penalty when the ball struck the hand of Chris Balderstone. 'I suppose that was the same as Saturday when they wanted a pen,' he said. 'That's right, Chris. Colours don't mean a thing,' I replied.

At the end I walked off, changed, and drove to Billingham to take my father home. Bob Stokoe had never uttered one solitary word of complaint to me. Neither had anyone else for that matter. But when I eventually got back to the farm my brother-in-law told me the telephone had never stopped ringing with Press men demanding my side of the controversy. What controversy?

It transpired that Stokoe, who had felt it unnecessary to say anything to my face, had felt no such compunction when it came to talking after I left. I digested his quotes with my breakfast the following morning.

'I don't think there can be any doubt that the appointment of these officials cost us the tie,' he said referring to me and my linesmen from Teesside Alan Jordan and Lol Douglas. 'They came out absolutely determined to be unbiased and they went too far the other way. We could have had at least one, and possibly three, penalties but the referee just didn't want to know.

'I believe that Sunderland were knocked out of the FA Cup because the referee had too much pressure on him. To get three officials in the replay from so near is absolutely ludicrous. The referee must have said to his linesmen before they went out "Hey watch it, we are on a hiding to nothing."

'I confess that I feel sorry for the referee in being given this responsibility. I am criticising the system.'

To make the whole thing more farcical Alan Ashman, who was supposed to have lodged two appeals, went on to suggest the exact opposite to Stokoe. I was supposed to have leaned towards Sunderland rather than away from them. Here were two professionals viewing the same game and coming to exactly opposing views which just happened to co-incide with the teams they were managing. And I was supposed to be biased!

Bob Stokoe's prolonged attack which, he said, he had considered very carefully, made me see red. I have never in my life been biased for or against any team. The only time that could possibly have a grain of truth in it is if Middlesbrough were involved and I have made certain that I have not been put in such a position. Sunderland mean no more or less to me than Torquay United, Liverpool or Inverness Thistle.

I objected strongly to Stokoe not only questioning my integrity but not having what I considered the guts to tell me to my face. He had left me to read all about it at home.

As for the attack on the FA he was way off the beam. They had not put pressure on me. They had given me the chance to refuse the matches and I had declined.

Jackie Milburn, the old Newcastle United and England centre-forward who is now a Press man, came to my aid. 'I've never seen a better performance by a referee,' he declared. 'Sunderland will have to look elsewhere for an excuse.'

Bob Stokoe and I never met up again for fifteen months until three days before I was due to take the 1975 FA Cup final. It was David Craig's testimonial at St James's Park and Newcastle United were playing Sunderland. After the game I was standing outside the guest room with Margaret talking to Stuart Loudon, a Football League linesman when Stokoe waved and nodded in my direction. 'Oh, aren't we speaking then?' he said on receiving no apparent acknowledgement and walked over. I was ready and gave him a right verbal going over for not telling me what he thought man to man but spilling it to the newspapers. 'Never ever do that again,' I finished up.

Margaret felt at the time that I had been a little harsh on him but I had lived for over a year with the taint of supposedly putting Sunderland out of the FA Cup and it hurt. What I did admire, belatedly, was Stokoe's willingness to stand there and let me have my say rather than walk away.

Our paths have crossed many times since and we have never had a wrong word.

6 . . . and referees

Without a shadow of doubt I sat at the knee and witnessed the art of my profession from two masters in Kevin Howley and Ken Dagnall. Yet, while their presence had a profound influence on my early career, I was to stay my own man. Kevin saw to that.

He was our celebrity on Teesside having earned a place in the record books in 1960 by becoming the youngest man to referee a Cup final when he took the Blackburn Rovers–Wolves game at Wembley ten days before his thirty-sixth birthday. That was indeed heady stuff to an up-and-coming youngster and on my promotion to the referees' list of the Football League I went to Kevin for advice.

Making the biggest step of my career required a certain change in style or at least so I thought. I needed to referee 'the Football League way' as opposed to the ordinary way and to find out precisely what that entailed I called on a man who had done it all.

Kevin's retort was hardly what I expected. 'The way you have refereed until now has got you on the League list so never ever change it,' he told me. Simple, straightforward words but I heartily recommend them to any young referee in the same position today. It is a myth to believe the Football League is a different world. Basics remain the same experience is the only real new commodity necessary.

When I was making progress we had another League

referee in the area who was forever moaning that we had no chance with someone of Kevin's calibre on our doorstep but I saw him more as a healthy challenge than a deterrent. I used to tell him: 'Get out, you're too old. I want your place.'

Kevin's reply was always the same: 'You'll have to flippin' well earn it first' and I think we were both pleased that when he retired from the international scene I took his place on it.

The man had always enthralled me at referees' society meetings with his stories of travel abroad and on my first trip overseas all my dreams were confirmed. I went with Ken Dagnall to Malmo in Sweden in 1966 for a European Cup match and I watched Ken's every move. He stood out as the epitome of what referees are all about. Immaculate both on and off the field, he was a referee's referee and I returned to England convinced that this was the life for me.

The Malmo Stadium had been built for the World Cup and it was a beautiful setting with flagpoles all the way round it. Ken put his hands on my shoulders and said: 'Take a good look. They are flying a Union Jack in your honour. Never forget that when you travel abroad.' There picked out against the vivid blue skyline three Union Jacks fluttered in the breeze as a mark of respect to the three match officials. My chest swelled with pride at the sight of it and that feeling of responsibility at representing your country in a foreign land has never ever left me. Basically it is what international football is all about.

Someone, somewhere had a lot of faith in me on that trip, because when the appointment was made I hadn't refereed in the Football League, yet I was the senior linesman and if something had happened to Ken Dagnall I would have been in the middle making my debut in a European Cup tie. Ken went on to take the FA Cup final at the end of

that season and now, like Kevin Howley, he's a Football
League assessor.

A couple of other referees from yesteryear who became
a little special to me are Jim Finney and Reg Leaf. I had the
privilege (and I mean privilege) of working with Jim only
once when I ran the line to him in the 1971 League Cup
final at Wembley but I never even saw Reg in action. I got
to know him through our Association conferences and he
was an inspiration to the younger set always ready to give
advice but only if it were sought. He would never thrust
his opinions down your throat. In the last eighteen months
our relationship has intensified through us both becoming
FA staff instructors.

In talking about my contemporaries I must stress that I
don't list them in order of preference. There is no such
thing for me – they are all, or have been, valued colleagues
and I give my personal views with respect to each and
every one.

Harold Hackney, now off the list through age, was a
character in the truest sense. From Barnsley, he was a typical
Yorkshireman who worked in the mining industry. A spade
was a shovel to Harold who became notorious for his
medicine bottle. He carried it in his bag and would take a
nip 'to keep out the cold tha' knows' before every game.

Once when he had a cup-tie at Bishop Auckland and I
had a free day I filled a hip flask and popped across to the
game. He was delighted to see me and even more delighted
to see my present. 'What would you have done if I hadn't
come?' I asked as he enjoyed a swig. With a huge smile he
rummaged in his hold-all and said triumphantly: 'I'd have
drunk this, lad' holding up a bottle of the medicinal.

I would call Harold a good general plodder and they are
the salt of the earth. I was convinced at one time that he
would become an international referee but a bad knee

injury put paid to that. In fact he was almost finished before his time because of it. He went off the Football League list and onto a contributory league to prove his fitness and did precisely that to bounce back again. I'm certain that Harold Hackney was the only man the Football League would have helped in such a way. They could have said 'hard lines' and promoted someone else in his place but they kept faith with him and waited for his recovery.

Harold lined for me three years ago in West Germany when FC Schalke 04 played RWD Molenbeek. I sent off the Schalke skipper and Harold, at the other end of the field, couldn't see what on earth was happening. Several seconds of craning his neck made little difference so Harold, aware that as a linesman on European duty he should know precisely what had taken place especially as it involved the home captain, decided drastic action was called for. Looking round for a lifeline his eyes descended on a West German policeman patrolling the touchline. In no time at all the said policeman had been dispatched round the field to ask the other linesman for full graphic details of the incident. Unorthodox but effective!

The role of a linesman in relation to a referee was amply demonstrated in that sending-off. I saw the Schalke captain foul an opponent who went down but then, out of my range of vision, he dug his boot into the man on the deck. I pulled out the yellow card for a caution on the original offence but my linesman, Joe Rees from Birmingham, flagged vigorously. When I ran across he told me: 'Pat, you must send him off' and proceeded to fill me in on what had happened. Joe could easily have chickened out – his value to me was his courage and teamwork.

Jack Taylor secured a special place for himself in the honours list with his selection to control the World Cup final in Munich in 1974. He did a tremendous job for the image of referees in general by having the courage and faith in himself to award a penalty against the host country, West Germany, in the first minute, but sadly in the next finals four years later he undid the good work by publicly condemning the actions of a colleague.

For a referee with the universal respect of Jack Taylor to go on television and suggest that another referee made a grave mistake involving the scoring of a goal during the World Cup finals is disastrous for our profession. But that's what Taylor did to Clive Thomas last year and, to make matters worse, Jack was totally wrong in his condemnation though because it came from such famous lips his words were believed by the layman.

The incident, you may remember, came during the Sweden–Brazil match in Argentina. Right at the death Brazil won a corner and as the ball came over Clive blew loudly for time and indicated it was all over. However the Brazilians managed to force the ball home to claim a goal which, of course, it wasn't.

The law states that a game is of ninety minutes duration and the only occasion that can be extended is for the taking of a penalty kick. Not for corners, free-kicks or the like. The match was over before Brazil 'scored' but Taylor, sitting in a television studio back home, stated that Thomas should have waited to see the outcome of the corner before blowing time.

His remarks reached us in South America and Clive was naturally perturbed at what he considered a personal attack. Evidently lots of referees took exception for the matter was actually raised at the Referees Association conference in Norwich while the World Cup was still going on.

It would have been bad enough for a player, manager or journalist to attack a referee when he was right but for another referee to do it hardly helped our cause. General criticism on a broad base is healthy but not an attack on a crucial decision during a game – the difference is enormous. It doesn't enhance our standing if we appear to be squabbling amongst ourselves on whether we are correct or not on a goal.

The original style of refereeing of Clive Thomas was certainly not mine though it obviously served him well enough not to hamper his progress. Clive flung cautions around like confetti, which was the sort of action to drive players and refs even further apart, and earned him the nickname Clive the Book. He thought his unbending attitude right, the majority of us thought it wrong.

Whether he enjoyed going to disciplinary committee sittings I don't know but the tale goes that once Denis Follows, then FA secretary, bumped into Clive at Lancaster Gate and asked if he could have a quick word. 'I've a personal hearing on,' replied Thomas. 'All right,' said Mr Follows. 'I'll see you in your office afterwards!' Certainly he was at headquarters so much that the FA staff thought he was employed full-time on the premises.

Clive is supposed to have changed since those days . . . seen the light, I believe the expression is. It is true that cautions no longer abound and he says he's more relaxed and happy now. Well, all I can say is that I came on the League list at the same time as you, Clive, and I've enjoyed every minute of it. What took you so long?

Much more important, perhaps, than style is attitude and here Clive seems not to want to mix. He has stated that attending meetings of the Association of Football League Referees and Linesmen is a waste of time as they don't talk about football and equally that he won't go along to referees' society meetings.

I find such isolation a tragedy because Clive Thomas has a wealth of experience and knowledge to pass on to others and only by attending our functions can he do that. We owe it to put something back into the game.

Okay, if our system is wrong let's change it not ignore it. If the AFLR and L don't talk about football then Clive had the perfect opportunity to change all that when he was asked to address the Association on his return from Argentina. He declined the invitation when he could have introduced the subject for himself and informed colleagues to their face about his ideas. People might have learned from his very presence.

Clive the Book he may be to the rest of the country but I call him Kick-start. Have you watched him start a game? I used to do that to a motor bike and it started but I never thought it would work with a human being!

Gimmicks, if that's the right word, feature in the make-up of one or two of our top whistlers. Clive has his dynamic kick to get his engine running; Roger Kirkpatrick and Maurice Fussey had the fiendish burst of acceleration to the by-line on giving a corner kick.

Roger, known as Mr Pickwick because of his roly-poly looks, would say when asked about his antics: 'I'm only a little bloke with short legs – I have to flippin' run like that.' In spite of his extrovert style he could control players and the fans had a lot of affection for him.

Gordon Hill, like Clive, earned himself a handle. He was 'the players' referee.' That was built mainly on the strength of being a talker during a game – I am, too, but there the similarity ends. Gordon liked to eff and blind in the belief that he was talking to players in their own language and therefore gaining their respect. I never swear on a football field or anywhere else for that matter. It's not being puritanical or anything. Just that I don't see the need, that's all.

To Gordon being liked was all important whereas I've

never gone out to win a popularity poll as a referee. Being popular is not my job – all I ask is respect. Gordon, I always felt, wanted to be the most popular guy with the players. It was the ultimate achievement in his eyes. Yet the way he went out to attain it greatly restricted his career. Building up communication and control largely on the quick four-lettered word dropped in the right place is hardly likely to work on the Continent and Gordon Hill never made the FIFA panel of referees.

He was never too happy on the odd occasion he reffed abroad and put it down to a language barrier yet, honestly, I don't think one exists. I've yet to find it if it does. Nowhere in the laws of the game does it say you must talk apart from asking a player his name on a caution so in theory at least language ought not to be a problem. I can't speak English, anyway, and if some player yaps at me in a foreign lingo I come out with a mouthful of Geordie which usually leaves him speechless.

My general thoughts on refereeing? Well, I don't believe it is our function to be the star of the show but equally I don't believe in the old criterion that a good referee is never seen. A good ref is seen when he has to be seen.

The chemistry of people is vastly different, of course, and leads to different styles. For example some refs are showmen because they are basically nervous and need to rush around gesticulating to relieve the inner tension.

I try to be less conspicuous. Gimmicks are not part of my make-up though I do have a habit of resting on my knee when I write but that's only to stop players seeing my hand shaking!

What I hate is to see referees point dramatically to the centre circle on awarding a goal, whirl round and hare off up the field. It's not only too flamboyant it's foolhardy. Think what can happen when the ball lands in the net. Opposing players can contest the goal, even fight over it. A linesman can flag for an infringement gone otherwise unnoticed. And there you are – fifty yards away with your back to all the action.

My response once a goal is scored is to quickly look to see if my linesman is happy and then to backpedal towards the centre never taking my eyes off the players in the goalmouth in case of any adverse reaction. I also insist that my linesman doesn't dash off up his line on the ball entering the net. Why should either of us make the other look foolish or give ourselves a long, embarrassing walk should consultation be necessary.

Humour is an essential ingredient in a referee and my name has helped tremendously in building up a rapport with the crowds. Partridge, as I always say, is there to be shot at!

Take the day Everton were playing at Blackpool. There was a lull in the game and suddenly this loud Scouse voice drifted from the paddock: 'Partridge, you want stuffing.' I just winked and put my thumb up as I ran past. Then at Carlisle on Boxing Day a wag yelled: 'I don't know – turkey yesterday and now Partridge today.'

Other shouts such as 'Get back in your pear tree' are commonplace but a lot of fun. The best way to defuse a situation, to prove you are human and can accept banter, is to respond to it. After all, the bloke has probably been under his wife's thumb all week and fancies having a go at somebody. A fellow at Bury was giving me a bit of stick in a more basic tongue than those I've already recalled and I shouted back with a wide grin: 'I bet you can't even spell it.' He saw the funny side and gave me a wave.

Occasionally the ladies get in on the act and at Grimsby a large woman behind one of the goals was going on and on. The ground wasn't exactly full and her voice seemed to echo round the place. I was dying to get up to her end of the field but play would never allow it. Then I got my chance – the ball ran out for a corner and as I signalled it I charged towards the wall. At the last moment I stuck my foot up to stop me in full flight, leaned over, and said: 'Give us a kiss, love.' She was struck dumb and the fans around her burst out laughing. I don't know if it was the thought of having to kiss a ref but there wasn't another peep out of her for the rest of the match.

7 Wembley

Wembley is Mecca to everybody in football in this country. Players, managers, coaches, referees . . . all dream of the day they make the long walk up the tunnel into the bright sunshine and electric atmosphere of a packed stadium on cup final afternoon.

Without such an experience no career is complete whatever other heights may have been scaled. That person remains unfulfilled. Therefore I consider myself more than a trifle fortunate to have officiated in no fewer than five Wembley finals, my first two as a linesman and the remaining three as the man in the middle.

I ran the line in the 1971 League Cup final between Spurs and Aston Villa and returned only weeks later to repeat the operation in the European Cup final when Ajax of Amsterdam took on Panathanaikos. The following season, 1972, saw me switched to the middle for the FA Trophy final between Stafford Rangers and Barnet then came the 1975 FA Cup final with West Ham and Fulham fighting it out and the 1978 League Cup final when the European champions Liverpool clashed with domestic champions Nottingham Forest.

Such an impressive list of games tells its own story and produces a fund of treasured memories for my old age but one match still stands out above all others. Not because the quality of the soccer was superior or because my personal performance produced the most satisfaction but, quite simply, because it was THE Cup final.

To us all there is really only one final – the FA Cup. It is not meant as a reflection on the others because every one is an immense honour but merely as a statement of fact. The FA Cup final is the one with the history and the tradition, all the pomp and the sense of occasion.

That is why 1975 meant so much to me especially as for two years I had been robbed of the great occasion by the unexpected success of my area teams in the North East. It had got to the situation where I wondered whether the gods had determined I would never get the big one. First Sunderland had reached Wembley against all the odds as a Second Division side in '73 and then Newcastle United made it the following season winning through every solitary round away from home.

Obviously I was a no hoper with clubs from my doorstep in the final and considering a referee has a strictly limited time in which to land his prize the apprehension was there.

Think of it this way – I have now been on the Football League list of referees for 13 years which means 13 FA Cup finals have been theoretically available to me. But out of those 13 the first four or five must be chalked off owing to my inexperience then, when geography suddenly takes a hand, the time factor is whittled right down. Unlike a player a referee cannot enhance his Wembley chances by a transfer to a successful club like Liverpool or Manchester United. Nor can he go back a second time.

The competition, too, is fierce. There are about twenty thousand referees of one kind or another in England and in the League's set-up there are nearly 90 referees on the full list, and approaching three hundred linesmen. Clawing to the top of that pile is the equivalent of climbing Everest.

After Sunderland's fairytale success Newcastle United

showed themselves as the next threat to my personal ambition and I vividly recall the day they really knocked all my dreams into a cocked hat.

It was in the sixth round and, having a rare Saturday afternoon off, I was busying myself round the farmyard with the portable radio tuned to the local station for all the latest football news. Newcastle were at home to Nottingham Forest and, with little more than twenty minutes to go, they were 3–1 down and playing with 10 men big Paddy Howard having been ordered off. I looked home and dry and I must admit to a little glow of satisfaction deep down inside at the thoughts of a major obstacle being removed from my Wembley path.

Off went the radio and I jumped into the car to pop down into Bishop Auckland for some supplies. The Post Office was my final port of call and as I was being served I casually asked: 'How did Newcastle get on then?'

'Won 4–3,' came the beaming reply, 'isn't it great?'

'Oh, yes,' I smiled weakly at our great North East success, 'just great.' I reeled out of the shop and drove home in a daze cursing Forest for not being able to finish off a team when they were 3–1 up and 11 men against 10 with no time at all to go. I had nothing against Newcastle personally, of course. It was merely that they stood between me and my aspirations and I am certain players feel the same sort of self preservation on cup days.

There had been more drama at St James's Park than I realised with a riot holding up play for several minutes before Newcastle came back with their three late goals to finish the match. Though the Football Association ordered a replay at Goodison Newcastle eliminated Forest at the third attempt and went on to beat Burnley in the semi-final to reach Wembley.

Even the following year Middlesbrough fleetingly

threatened to make it a North Eastern hat-trick of final appearances battling through to the sixth round before being beaten. From that moment on I felt that, surely, this was to be my year and at precisely 20 minutes to two on Monday, March 10 my prayers were answered. The phone rang and when I answered it Reg Paine, the referees' secretary of the FA, asked: 'What are you doing on May the third?' I admit that Margaret and I shed a few tears of joy at the news. My appointment was one of the earliest ever made for the FA Cup final and there were still five clubs involved in the competition at the time including not-so-far-away Leeds United.

Reg's lovely phone call was the signal for all hell to be let loose. I had automatically become the centre of attraction for the media and the calls for stories poured in punctuated regularly by friends showering me with congratulations. Photographers navigated their way to our farm from all points of the compass and I was pictured humping bales of hay and feeding cows until the happy smile froze on my face. Throughout it all was the uneasy feeling that time was slipping by unnoticed and I had the West Riding Senior Cup final to referee at Bradford that night.

Eventually I slipped away about quarter past four pausing only to grab my grip as I sprinted for the car. On arrival at Bradford I settled into the dressing-room and prepared to change at about five past seven – twenty five minutes before kick-off. I have never been one to change early like some players and officials and in my book I had plenty of time.

When I came to open my grip all there was inside were my boots and box of tricks where I keep my whistle and the like. 'Come on, you jokers. Where's my gear?' I said turning to my linesmen who were already in black and tying their laces. We have our comedians and it wouldn't have been the first time my stuff was nicked and dumped behind the toilets or in some equally unlikely place. Only this time the genuine look of surprise on their faces told me a different tale. This was no joke.

I had taken off in all the chaos without the bulk of my kit and now there was less than twenty minutes to go before kick-off and I could hear the noise of the crowd above my head. It was time to panic – but I remembered that a local ref was sitting in the guest room. He could be my lifeline if I could reach him. A search was launched, he was located, and I demanded to know if he had his kit with him.

'Who's cried off?' he inquired, his face lighting up in anticipation of a late call to duty. No one, I told him, but where is the gear? It was in his car outside still damp and crumpled from a game the previous day. Mess or not to me it was the finest suit of clothes money could buy and minutes later I emerged from the tunnel . . . the newly appointed FA Cup final referee in an ill fitting shirt and wet, cramped shorts tucked in and held together by safety pins!

My official letter from the Football Association was dated April 14 and underlined how, on occasions, that great institution can be outdated. Part of the letter warned me not to appear on the stage of a music hall prior to the final. I ask you – I know we are considered by some to be comedians but a music hall act. Surely not.

The letter, signed by secretary Ted Croker, told me of the appointment, requested my acceptance by return of post, then went on :

Rule 23 of the Challenge Cup Competition provides that the Referee is entitled to a fee of £15.75 and a souvenir medal which will be presented to you by the Chief Guest at the conclusion of the game.

I have to draw your attention to the following Resolution of the Council:

'That the Secretary be instructed to inform the Final Tie Officials that the Council does not consider it consistent with the dignity of the officials that they should appear in Cinema Films or on the stage of any Music Hall, Theatre, or place of entertainment for the purpose of being presented with a whistle or other token in connection with the Final Tie.'

The fee of £15.75 may seem a pittance when you consider what players can make plus the fact that we are performing before 100,000 people live and literally millions more on television throughout the world and obviously it is but the cash is literally the last thought that entered my head. It might sound glib but I would have reffed the game for nothing. Money mattered not one jot though the medal did – a beautiful golden souvenir with a referee, ball under one arm, depicted leaning on the FA crest.

Less than a week after that communique from the Football Association a second letter from them landed me in a pre-match row over my Wembley outfit with me refusing to toe the official party line.

This one read:

Dear Sir,

Further to our previous correspondence I have to inform you that arrangements have been made with Messrs Mansfield-Banbury to supply you with a Referee's outfit. I presume that you will be quite happy to accept this and we have advised the Company of your name and address so that they may communicate with you regarding your measurements etc.

Yours faithfully,
R A Paine.
For the secretary.

That presumption of the FA had also been assumed by the managing director of the sportswear firm concerned who had, in fact, beaten the FA to the punch in writing to me asking for my measurements.

I was annoyed that everyone should take it as read that having been given the Cup final I would automatically jump full of gratitude into whatever gear was offered. I had worn Umbro International for a considerable while and the firm had been good to me. I liked their stuff, I felt comfortable in it, and I was not about to jettison them now just before I handled the biggest game of the season. Loyalty, I felt, still counted for something in this world.

Politely I informed both the FA and Mansfield-Banbury of my decision. The company were less than pleased. At first they pointed out that it was their custom to dress all the Cup final match officials and when that didn't work they asked if they could send me a full kit anyway even if I left it at home.

I recognised the advertising possibilities of that one with the firm still being able to say, quite justifiably if they wished, that they supplied all three Wembley officials with match-day gear and consequently I refused.

It was something of a political storm in a teacup but I stuck to my guns and the official photograph underlines the point. My outfit is jet black while the linesmen on either side of me are dressed in much lighter shirts and shorts. I moved quietly to one side out of camera shot while the advertising pics were taken for Mansfield-Banbury. It all happened in front of the Royal Box but I doubt if more than a handful of folk realised what was going on.

My linesmen were Ron Challis, an experienced Football League referee from Tonbridge, and George Holt of Birmingham who has since retired. I was thrilled to bits to have the pair of them especially Ron who the previous season had almost resigned because he was getting so little enjoyment out of the game. He had gone as far as sounding out a few of us about his intentions and it was well known on the referees' grapevine that Ron Challis was about to quit.

Fortunately he stayed on, got the lift of running the line in the Cup final, and is one of our outstanding referees today.

There is a school of thought, mind you, that referees should not be appointed to run the line in top games. The reason is that lack of recent experience of such duties is supposed to be a major drawback. It is one Gordon Hill, for example, feels strongly about but I disagree with him all the way.

Hill is wrong in his reasoning and his conclusion. It is all a question of attitude not recent experience. Sometimes a senior ref taking a line will think it below his dignity. He feels inferior and believes that it should be him and not the other fellow out there in the middle.

That sort of bloke will kill the game for you because, make no mistake about it, you are only as good as your linesmen. If they blow it you are in big trouble. There is no way that twenty-two players will dig you out if your own mates put you in the mire.

Yet a senior referee with the right attitude taking a line for you can be a huge advantage. A lot disagree with me but I believe that to run a line correctly is more difficult than to referee. The linesman has to keep an eye not only on play but on the last line of defence as well for offsides and so much scorn is poured upon him by players and spectators if he waves it wrongly.

Ron Challis took the right attitude to Wembley and a couple of years later my point about senior refs on the line was backed to such an extent I reported it to our Association.

The occasion was the European Cup-Winners' Cup final in Amsterdam when Ken Burns was the senior ref appointed to the line by UEFA and Arthur Jones the other linesman appointed by the FA. Here were two linesmen with between twenty and twenty-five years experience as League referees behind them who had little experience with the flag yet their attitude was perfect and I couldn't praise them enough.

Indeed some time later at our Association of League Referees and Linesmen's banquet when it is customary for all officials honoured that year to receive their gifts I asked our president, Ray Tinkler, if we could reverse the procedure for this particular final and send the two linesmen up first then the referee.

After Ken and Arthur had received their applause it was my turn and in my address to my colleagues I said: 'The myth that referees can't run the line has now been killed off for ever. It was finally killed in Amsterdam by Ken Burns and Arthur Jones. I couldn't have picked two linesmen who would have done a better job.'

The formation of that third team of referee and linesmen is something which is handled very delicately by the Football Association. It is not widely known but it is a fact that when a referee gets a game abroad Reg Paine will ring and say : 'We are thinking of appointing so-and-so and so-and-so. Have you any objections?' If you have then that person will be dropped from the trip without anyone knowing about it and he will get the next one available.

The reason is that while it may be possible for three people to work together and get through 90 minutes it is a vastly different proposition to live in one another's pockets for four days travelling abroad. Any personal friction then and the whole operation can fall apart. It is a smooth piece of behind-the-scenes checking by the FA which guarantees harmony.

But I digress a little from the FA Cup final. My build-up after a short trip to Jersey and one to Russia to handle the Dynamo Kiev–PSV Eindhoven Cup-winners' Cup semi-final went like this: SATURDAY – York City v Oldham; MONDAY – Blackburn Rovers v Wrexham; WEDNESDAY – David Craig's testimonial match at Newcastle; THURSDAY – travel to London for the Football Writers' Association dinner; FRIDAY – the eve-of-the-final Referees' Rally.

Three matches and two dinners might appear to be a hectic way to prepare for the greatest moment of your life but I like it that way. Nice and busy.

On the big day the FA drove the four of us (three officials plus reserve linesman Colin Mallett) to Wembley in a huge limousine for lunch. I skipped it having only a coffee and a sandwich and insisting on my two linesmen reporting to the dressing-room at 12.30 prompt. I was determined that no one would be nervous. We could mar the final if we froze and as this was my fourth visit to Wembley I felt it was up to me to ease the situation.

We went out onto the pitch twenty or twenty-five minutes before the gates were opened and walked round getting used to the vastness of it all and chatting to the stewards. Slowly Wembley began filling up and we were still there on the turf. I signed a few autographs and talked to a few fans. It was all informal, almost casual.

But I knew what I was doing. It was all pre-planned and working like a charm. Ron Challis and George Holt had watched the build-up and they were prepared for that 100,000 crowd. We didn't hide in the dressing-room and then walk out cold to be hit – bang – by the noise and the atmosphere.

Perhaps I played it too cool for some because at two o'clock the FA officials began to flap at my walkabout. Reg Paine, whose duty it was to look after us for the day, and

Dickie Bird, who leads out the procession, both inquired anxiously if I was going to get changed.

The match itself was a dream to handle. Fulham boss Alec Stock had gone on record as saying: 'Pat Partridge will have the easiest game of his life. All he'll have to do is blow his whistle and come and sit with me.' He was right.

There wasn't a bad foul in the game, the two goals by Alan Taylor which won West Ham the Cup were clean, and the Football Association Year Book later recorded: 'Pat Partridge, an inconspicuous but highly efficient referee, deserves great credit for his handling of the game from start to finish. On at least a dozen occasions he successfully exploited the advantage rule and it was largely due to him that, for what must have been the first time ever in a Cup final, neither trainer set foot on the pitch, an achievement for which all concerned deserve congratulations.'

After the game Ron Challis said: 'Where do you keep it?' and when I asked what on earth he was talking about he replied: 'The advantage clause because, boy, you use it well.'

More often than not referees receive criticism rather than praise and consequently we tend to expect little else but it is nice on occasions to get a bouquet and I must say I was pleased deep down inside that my day had gone off so well. Even a top Fleet Street journalist, known as something of a hatchet man, made me his man of the match ahead of his top players Alan Taylor and Bobby Moore.

I remember one amusing incident at the West Ham banquet (we went on to the Fulham shindig later) when their centre-half Tommy Taylor approached me with a puzzled look on his face. 'Tell me, Pat, what's all this on-your-bike stuff?' he said. 'I'm a ruddy footballer not a Tour of France cyclist.'

I suppose to a Cockney such Geordie slang sounds weird

but it's my way of telling any player chasing me to moan about a decision that he would be better off disappearing. Sharpish.

A slightly sour note crept in on my return home when the following letter dated May 13 arrived from the FA:

Dear Mr Partridge,

I have received an account from the Great Western Royal Hotel in respect of your stay over the period of the Cup Final a copy of which is attached.

I understand that The Football Association is only responsible for the cost of the hotel for the nights of 2nd and 3rd May. I should be grateful therefore if you would reimburse The Football Association with the sum of £15.33 or, alternatively, inform me of any reason for the Association paying for the costs relating to 1st May.

> Yours sincerely,
> G Woodward.
> Accountant.

My first reaction was one of aggravation. It seemed to me that the FA were penny pinching by asking their top match official for £15.33 which, taken off his match fee of £15.75 meant he had refereed the Cup final for forty-two pence. On reflection, however, the FA were within their rights. I knew the rules when I started and I had stayed an extra night to attend the Football Writers' Association dinner. Perhaps if I had spoken to Ted Croker it would have been different but the accounts department were only doing their job. So I coughed up and shut up.

All the same should anyone ever question a referee's devotion to his job I have the perfect answer. I took charge of the Football Association's showpiece for a mere forty-two pence!

All in all the FA Cup final had been perfect – so good, in fact, that even if referees in modern times were occasionally asked to do a second final I would be apprehensive to accept. It could never be quite the same again.

Wembley has been good to me. Five times I have trodden that famous turf without one controversial incident. When a final did cough up such a moment it was in a replay at Old Trafford. That was last year when I awarded Nottingham Forest the penalty which won them the League Cup against Liverpool and sparked off a row over whether the foul was inside the box or not.

My dear friend Jim Finney had taken the League Cup final seven years earlier when I was on the line and he was due to handle the European Cup final shortly afterwards but suffered horrific injuries in a car crash on his way to a Football League game and Jack Taylor deputised at Wembley. Kevin Howley and I were on the line.

Jim turned up for the game bent double by the mass of stitches which held his body together after a long and complicated operation. There were tears in my eyes at the sight of such a lovely man in such obvious distress on what should have been his day. I always admired him both as a ref and as a person and during his long convalescence I gave him a tinkle and announced: 'I'll give you a hand with the garden sometime, Jim.' You should have seen his face the next day when I turned up on the doorstep and said: 'Come on, mate. Where's the spade?' We were on our way on holiday and popped in to surprise him.

Ajax won the European Cup 2–0 and England had her first real look at a young man who was to dominate the world scene – Johann Cruyff. And I had my first taste of that unique Continental atmosphere with rockets shooting off everywhere. One landed at my feet and I thought: 'My God. It's got my name on it.' But I survived and on the way up to the Royal Box for the presentations both the Dutch and Greek fans smothered us in kisses. It's not every day the ref and linesmen are so well received at the end of the game.

George Best – 'Don't be a silly little devil.'

Pat walks out with his linesmen Brian Langford (on the left) and Roger Kirkpatrick for a European Cup tie in Cologne in 1978. The Cologne players follow.

Above: At the centre of things. Brazil's skipper Roberto Rivelino (right) shakes hands with France's captain before an international in Paris.

Below left: It's like this, ref. A mud-splattered Archie Gemmill pleads his case.

Below right: Phew. How to get browned off during a football match.

Look at the surface of the pitch – it's soccer in Kuwait. Acrobats and all.

A study in expressions from the 1977/78 derby match between Newcastle United and Sunderland at St James's Park with Newcastle captain Terry Hibbitt all arms.

Above: Famous faces — Holland captain Cruyff and Poland's skipper Deyna.

Below: It's different from Anfield or Old Trafford, isn't it? Pat lines in the Horden Colliery v Whitby Town match as training for the World Cup finals in Argentina.

World Cup finals in Argentina. Pat looks on with Brazilian referee Arnaldo Coelho as the France v Hungary match at last gets under way forty minutes late.

Above: What about the fellow with the funny haircut on the extreme right? The final of the Ashmore Benson Departmental Cup between the Foundry and the Fitting Shop in May 1957.

Below: Gordon Lee — 'watch this referee, he's going to make it,' he said.

Above: Pat Partridge with some of his souvenirs in his study.

Below left: Walking away from it — Holland v Poland in Warsaw.

Below right: Jack Charlton — 'his goal-line trick was a tremendous tactic'.

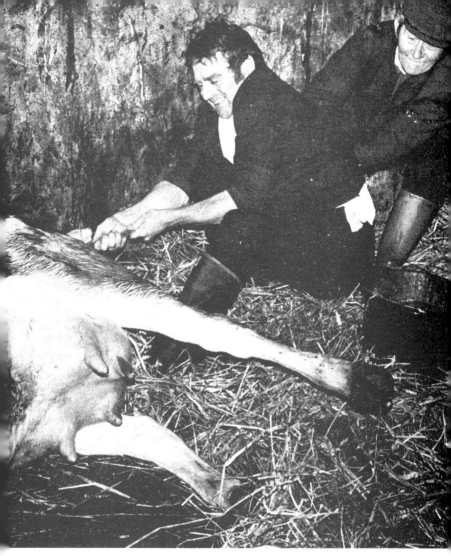

Above left: The World Cup referees after a training session in Argentina.

Below left: Wilf Smith and Pat try eating with chopsticks during Coventry City's tour of Japan.

Above: Calving on the farm with my father-in-law. A real sweat.

Above: The car number plate says it all . . . when a Football League referee must stop whistling.

Below: The start of the second half of this match in India is held up — while the steam-roller trundles off after rolling the pitch at Darjeeling.

Gordon Banks – reported over the jersey he was wearing.

Above: Now then . . . Pat Partridge talks to Sunderland's Bob Lee.

Below: Brian Clough — a man of contradictions who is great with kids.

Above: Hot in pursuit. David Fairclough, supported by Ian Callaghan, breaks away for Liverpool during the 1978 League Cup Final against Nottingham Forest.

Below: Confrontation. Pat Partridge and Liverpool skipper Emlyn Hughes during the 1978 League Cup Final.

Above: Let him call. Emlyn Hughes indicates to Nottingham Forest captain John McGovern as Pat holds the coin at the start of the 1978 League Cup Final.

Below: Look — now it's time. Pat with the Anderlecht No 8 in the European Cup winners' Cup Final of 1977.

Above: Here we come! Anderlecht v HSV Hamburg in the 1977 European Cup-winners' Cup Final.

Below: With the Royal Box in the background Pat chats with skippers Billy Bonds of West Ham (left) and Fulham's Alan Mullery at the start of the 1975 FA Cup Final at Wembley.

Ouch! Ally Brown is down and his West Brom team-mates Derek Statham and Willie Johnston console him as Pat waves on the coach to revive the stricken striker.

8   World Cup

Eleven World Cup matches ending amid the splendour of the eleventh World Cup finals in South America was as neat a package as I could have asked for. In the space of almost six years I had quietly and patiently climbed the ladder of soccer's most prestigious international tournament rung by rung to reach Argentina.

The World Cup was conceived in France, the dream of Jules Rimet, after whom the first trophy was eventually named, and Henri Delavnay and was given birth in Uruguay in 1930. The beginnings were relatively humble but exciting with scores of packet boats ferrying fans across the River Plate to Montevideo for the final between intense rivals Uruguay and Argentina which the host country won 4–2.

John Langenus, the celebrated Belgian referee who officiated, whatever the heat, in cap and plus fours, was the centrepiece not only of the final but the whole tournament having earlier been involved in a rather unusual exchange with the medical attendant of the American team. Upon giving a freekick to the opposition Langenus was verbally assaulted by the American gentleman who concluded his argument by flinging his box of medicines to the ground. The box burst open, various bottles smashed including one full of chloroform, and its fumes rose to overpower the American who had to be helped from the field. The World Cup was truly launched with referees appropriately at the focal point.

Almost half a century later the World Cup was to be held in the country of those first beaten finalists who were to go one better at long last and claim the trophy as their own. But, as with all finals, the path is long and arduous. Teams from the four corners of the globe do battle for two years to even reach the stage of real confrontation and referees likewise must qualify.

I had flirted fleetingly with the World Cup before the '74 finals in West Germany when I ran the line in the Belgium v Holland qualifier which was, incidentally, Keith Walker's last international which he handled splendidly. However my apprenticeship for Argentina was much more thorough – probably the most thorough of all referees, in fact. I was involved in no fewer than seven qualifying matches including a whistle stop fifteen days in Doha on the Gulf where a full group comprising of Bahrain, Kuwait and Qatar decided their fate in shortened form.

Four referees were flown in from Italy, West Germany, Switzerland and England to share all match duties on a rota basis and we shuffled between line and middle.

The consensus of opinion at this stage (around March, 1977) was that the choice of our representative for the finals lay between myself and Ken Burns, president of the Referees Association. England have four representatives on the senior FIFA list and therefore theoretically four men were in with a shout but Ken and I were by far the most experienced ones getting games regularly in Europe which is something taken into account along with World Cup qualifying matches and internationals.

Two months after my return from Middle East patrol Ken lined for me in the European Cup-winners' Cup final. In the dressing-room at the end he held out his hand and said: 'There's only one man for Argentina now. Well done.' It was a nice gesture from a friend as well as a rival but that's the kind of bloke Ken is.

The exceptionally high stakes played for at every World Cup table were amply demonstrated even before setting out for Latin America. Holland received her passport by beating Belgium 1–0 but the party was full of faces pleading with their greatest player, Johann Cruyff, not to retire before Argentina in favour of a TV commentary chair. He sat, almost kinglike, through the entire night refusing to relent despite many persuasive tongues and flowing wine – an intriguing sight. The plea failed amid national mourning yet, ironically, Holland still reached the River Plate final itself.

If the stake then was a footballer of unique talent on other occasions it was gold. Sacks full of it.

Iran played the Republic of Korea in Teheran and one of their officials, quizzed by a journalist, stated almost off-handedly that the players were on five million American dollars to reach Argentina. The look on the face of the questioner was one of such amazement that it prompted the response: 'I will repeat it for you. You heard correctly – five million American dollars.'

Iran, hardly a soccer nation to stir the imagination, could still command such startling rewards at such an early stage of the competition but they produced enough evidence in the game I handled, coming back from two down to two all, that I was prompted to warn a Scottish newspaperman who phoned me on my return: 'Be careful, don't under-estimate them. They can play a bit and they are organised.' Iran went on to shake the world drawing 1–1 with Scotland.

FIFA's list of match officials was drawn up in Zurich in mid February three months before all were due to arrive in Buenos Aires. There were thirty-two referees and three Argentinians to act as linesmen and linesmen only. I was in and so were Clive Thomas representing Wales and Scotland's John Gordon.

A four-page letter from the FIFA secretary Dr Kaser set out no fewer than sixteen points which all referees had to adhere to. Point nine said: 'Thorough physical training is compulsory and the referees must report to Argentina in the best possible physical condition. Fitness tests will be made during the conference in Buenos Aires.' That was no problem. I keep fit by utilising the heavy work on the farm to build me up and I have various distances paced out on the poles in the fields to act as a cross-country running course.

Fitness was an obvious requirement but what was not generally known was the final point, sixteen, which was prefixed by the words 'Very important' and stated: 'All selected referees must be given an opportunity to act also as linesmen in their national competitions as each referee may also be appointed as a linesman during the final competition.' That undertaking, along with the others, was signed not only by me but by the Football Association yet when I attempted to stick by the demand a lot of folk thought I was indulging in a neat little gimmick aimed at promoting PP.

What happened, you see, was that I turned to my old stamping ground, the Northern League, to do my bit on the line. Their secretary Gordon Nicholson was extremely helpful when I asked if I could intrude. 'How many games do you want?' he replied. I had been the first ref to jump direct from the Northern League onto the League list and consequently was welcomed back like the prodigal son.

My two soccer jobs went together nicely hand in hand. I reffed in the Football League on a Saturday and lined in the Northern League in midweek. Authority was happy but the extremes of a World Cup whistler taking the flag in non-league matches was too good for the media to miss out on. Cameras from both the BBC and Independent Television descended upon various Durham pit villages to record the event going into grounds to look at a linesman where they had never gone to look at a game. No wonder some thought it all a gimmick.

Preparations over, I jetted out to Buenos Aires on the same plane as John Gordon and Jack Mowat, Scotland's former international referee who had the legendary European Cup final between Real Madrid and Eintracht Frankfurt a film of which I must have seen at least twenty times at various refs' meetings. Jack is a member of the FIFA referees committee and as such had been our supremo during my fortnight on World Cup duty in the Middle East.

I can't speak for either John or Jack but my thoughts on that long flight strayed repeatedly to what lay ahead. I have always made it a strict rule when travelling abroad not to prejudge a country either on what other people have told me or what I have read. They can be biased and damning a place before seeing it is dangerous. All the same Argentina had appeared sinister in the extreme, a politically devastated country torn apart by kidnappings and other guerilla activities. There had even been talk of taking the World Cup from them for security reasons and in the end when they retained the world spotlight the resultant military measures were reckoned to be suffocating. Life was lived in a straitjacket, it was said.

All thirty-two referees were housed in the Carlton Hotel slap bang in the centre of Buenos Aires for the full five weeks of our stay and a strong security operation was naturally mounted. We were the middle men, literally, in the world's greatest show and as such potential targets either for nuts who might disagree with an offside decision or big-time gamblers who felt our influence could be beneficial to their financial future. That had to be the official thinking anyway.

Guys walked round the hotel lobby in sports coats and slacks but it was easy to ascertain that they were security guards. The slight bulge of a hand gun in every case was the giveaway.

Their efficiency was never in doubt from the second day onwards as far as I was concerned. A reporter from the Beeb Jim Rosentall came round to see me and, after a coffee in the foyer, asked if he could tape a short interview to which I agreed. We walked to the lifts with not a soul in sight, entered, and pressed the button for the seventh floor to go to my room. Without warning a hand shot out to prevent the lift doors from closing. It was two burly security guards.

We were both wearing our official creditations – me as a referee and he as a Pressman – but it made little difference. What's in the box, they demanded eyeing the tape recorder slung over my interviewer's shoulder. Where are you going? Why? The eyes were narrowed in suspicion. I'm not sure which of us had to change underpants first!

The interpreter, a charming girl called Marie, eventually arrived on the scene to defuse things and explain: 'We are doing this for your own good. We want to prove to you that we are efficient hosts.' All of us got to know the security men pretty well after that and they were great fellas. We ended up frisking them to make sure they were armed and larking about with their peashooters like a bunch of kids let loose in a fantasy world.

The surveillance was neither continuous nor objectionable. Far from it – it was nice and reassuring to have such people on your side. If any of us went out shopping, for example, no guards accompanied us but if we ever left the hotel on official business then it was different. We were under protection.

Physical training sessions were arranged daily by Roger

Quinche, a member of the FIFA technical committee from Switzerland. We had the full use of the River Plate Stadium and the military academy which was resplendent with restaurant, sauna bath and swimming pool, and vast parkland was just fifteen minutes away from the hotel. The programme was comprehensive and varied. We even danced to a mouth organ if you can imagine me tripping the light fantastic.

The Argentinians gave us virtually everything we wanted. They are a proud nation, they realised they were under the microscope, and their efforts were such that they should have received a public apology in all the world's newspapers at the end of the tournament for the scare stories which were circulated without foundation.

The only thing they got wrong was the fog. They legislated for everything else. The system was that we remained at base and flew from BA to all our matches which was fine until the fog descended as it did when I was due in Mendoza for the Peru–Poland game. Alternative travel was by rail and I left the capital at half past nine of the Friday night arriving at my destination at quarter past five the following afternoon. That's almost twenty four hours on a train to cover a distance the equivalent of Newcastle to London which can be done in three hours if you get the high-speed Flying Scot.

There were thirty-two referees for thirty-eight games which meant that if one or two got a couple of matches it was possible never to referee a game at all. Nonetheless I was very, very proud to be the only person from England at any level to take part in the World Cup and if I could have worn a huge Union Jack on my back I would have. The feeling of patriotism was so strong that I would gladly have sold programmes or been a ball boy if necessary. As it was I refereed one match and was linesman in another two, all of which produced some outstanding feature.

I took the line to Portuguese ref Antonio Jose da Silva Garrido (how's that for a handle?) in Argentina's opening match against Hungary in the multi-tiered River Plate Stadium. It was filled to capacity – 77,260 – and it was the introduction to all Europeans of the fascinating ticker tape welcome afforded Argentina's heroes with confetti cascading down from the terraces on sight of the blue and white shirts. The noise was unbelievable . . . I've never worked in an atmosphere quite like it either before or since. It wasn't frightening, more lifting. Stimulating.

Only three players were sent off during the entire World Cup and two were in this match which Argentina won 2–1. Hungarians Andras Torocsik and Tibor Nyilasi, both previously cautioned, were dismissed in the closing stages for bad tackles. From my position the referee was dead right and he never hesitated. The Hungarians lost their heads and had to go.

Hungary behaved themselves a lot better eight days later in Mar del Plata when they opposed France but, despite all the meticulous preparation by FIFA, there was still a slip up and the game actually kicked off forty minutes late. Referee Arnaldo Coelho of Brazil, Chile's Juan Silvagno and myself were in the dressing-room when the word was passed to us just before the scheduled start that there could be a problem. Investigation confirmed the worst . . . both sides were wearing identical shirts.

How that could possibly happen in the World Cup finals with colour charts drawn up weeks in advance is almost beyond comprehension but happen it had. It was France's fault, they admitted that, and Jack Mowat as the official referee observer was dispatched to sort it all out. The aggravation was heightened by the TV crews who were due to beam the match back to Europe and who with the time differences had a big problem already and a tight time schedule to keep. Eventually a set of shirts were borrowed from a local club and the game got under way.

It turned out to be one of the best of the tournament even though neither side progressed beyond the first round. The football was brilliant and the excitement intense. France swept into a 3–1 interval lead which was confidently expected to be doubled in the second-half. Surprisingly there were no more goals but the tempo never dropped for a second. A wonderful advertisement for the World Cup.

There is no way I can leave that game without a special mention of the referee Coelho. He was already a close friend of mine having looked after me when I was invited to Rio for a month before the 1974 World Cup finals.

Brazil work it whereby if the finals are to be held in South America they go on a European tour to get used to the 'unknown' but if it is the other way round they invite European teams and referees to their country for a series of games.

Coelho took me under his wing and it was an enlightening experience to see how the other half live. He is one of his country's biggest stars feted wherever he goes. His own physio to attend him before games, a swish pad in town, the lot. He's even on a percentage of the gate at some matches which makes him a rich man. It's all legitimate . . . hardly the life of the poor old English ref.

Obviously my biggest memory was the game I got in the middle, Peru v Poland in Mendoza in the second series of matches. Peru had caught everyone's attention with their flamboyant style of play, rhythmic and almost uninhibited. Poland possessed the household names like their big, blond centre back Gorgon, skipper Deyna who was later to sign for Manchester City, Lato and Lubanski.

But it was to be Peru's goalkeeper Ramon Quiroga, out-standing in the defeat of Scotland, who was to steal the show. He was aptly nicknamed El Loco, the Madman.

Quiroga kept charging out of his goal to make tackles, sometimes by the halfway line. I had never seen anything like it in twenty-five years of refereeing even in the parks. The first time I noticed him out of the corner of my eye I could just see a blue blur near the centre circle. 'Oh, no. There's a spectator on the pitch,' I thought. Then I realised it was El Loco. Twice he made really good tackles like a midfield ball winner but in the second-half he steamed out and pulled down Lato in his opponent's half!

He picked himself up, ran away two or three yards, and then bowed low in front of me. The crowd were beside themselves with laughter and I was also in kinks but I still had to give him the yellow card for ungentlemanly be-haviour. If I had let him get away with it other players who use similar tactics would be entitled to say: 'Hold on a minute, ref – look what you allowed that character to do in the World Cup.' Players expect a ref to have a sense of humour and it is important that they do but it doesn't mean using a laugh or a joke to shirk your res-ponsibility.

At the end of the game El Loco waited for me and walked off with his arm round my shoulder. There was no language barrier between us. We had both understood each other perfectly throughout.

The match, which Poland won through a second-half goal from Szarmach, didn't stand out from a footballing point of view. There were too many stops and starts but for the sheer experience it was special.

Clive Thomas was one of my linesmen ('I don't know who's been made to suffer – me or you, Pat,' he grinned on hearing the news) and it might interest the refereeing fraternity to know that even Clive came in for corners. For the uninitiated that means he followed my preference of the linesman walking up the goal-line to watch for any encroachment. Clive is one of the few referees who insists his linesman stands behind the flag on corners.

Prior to leaving for the World Cup I had stated how I would love to see Scotland win the trophy to boost British soccer. With so many players out of the English League we could all have basked in the glory for years. Instead we know what happened . . . humiliation, elimination and a drug scandal.

Naturally I had little to do with the Scottish party during their participation in the tournament. I saw only snippets of their games on television but Ron Greenwood, Dave Sexton and I had dinner with Martin Buchan on the eve of their return home. Other players were in the restaurant and the mood was dark. What had happened had bitten deep into the more sedate professionals like Buchan and they knew what waited for them at home. I felt deeply sorry for the caring.

Defeat was bad enough but the Willie Johnston affair was a darned sight worse. If anyone had said to me before Argentina that some British players took drugs I would have said: 'No way.' I would have scoffed at even the merest suggestion.

It was made even more tragic because everything had been spelled out crystal clear at a meeting called by the FIFA executive committee at the Sheraton Hotel the day before the opening game. All delegation heads of the sixteen competing nations and all referees were present and the FIFA medical experts went to great lengths on the use of drugs. All were listed without exception and for every drug prohibited a couple were named which were totally acceptable. The delegates were informed precisely how the ballot of players for tests would work and the consequences of a test proving positive.

Scotland, remembering that meeting, must at least be complimented on sending Willie Johnston straight home and not waiting for FIFA to act. They quelled a much bigger storm by doing so.

CONCLUSIONS.

Looking back over the five weeks of my stay in Argentina it is simpler to list the achievements or otherwise of this complex competition in straightforward fashion. So here goes:

1. Retaliation was down to a minimum which was perhaps a pleasant surprise considering the high stakes.

2. There was little dissent and games were hardly ever held up for treatment of players.

3. Players adhered to the ten-yard law on free-kicks allowing them to be taken quickly though such was the accuracy of the specialists that even if Wimpey's had built a brick wall the ball would have been bent round that as well.

4. From the refereeing and lining point of view the general standard was good. However some referees had obviously not acted on the FIFA instruction to get in some practice as a linesman before leaving home. We let ourselves down somewhat in this department.

5. The referees' headquarters were badly situated in the centre of a noisy, bustling city. Whenever Argentina played we were to get no sleep as supporters marched through the streets in triumph. Even grandmothers and grandfathers paraded clashing pots and pans together. The din was awful if the spirit friendly. General organisation, however, was outstanding.

6. Crowd behaviour. One of the great achievements of the eleventh World Cup finals. During the whole of my time in Argentina I never saw a drunk yet beer was sold openly not only in the supermarkets but in the football stadiums as well. Rival supporters mixed freely extending the open hand of welcome rather than the clenched fist and national anthems were treated with the respect they deserve. It saddens me to hear God Save the Queen drowned at Wembley.

7. Friendship, the international sporting language, was exercised at all levels from the top to the person in the street. Let me give you just two of many examples at each end of the spectrum.

Out for a stroll with one of the Argentinian linesmen, we got hemmed in by the exuberant, noisy hordes celebrating another local victory and took refuge in a shop doorway. Conversation was in broken Spanish (me) and broken English (him). Three or four young girls watched us with obvious curiosity edging closer to listen until one piped up with a question about England. Things developed rapidly and went on for some twenty minutes with my inquisitor translating into Spanish every so often for the benefit of her eager-faced friends. When it was time to go she shyly took her Girl Guides badge out of her lapel and offered me it. As I bent down to take it she flung her arms round my neck and gave me a big kiss. 'That is for you to remember us all when you go home,' she said beaming. I've still got the badge in my study.

Kindness equally touching was shown at the official farewell dinner attended by President Videla and every World Cup VIP still in Buenos Aires. A couple of days earlier a letter had arrived from home asking if I could possibly get two Brazilian badges for my friend's sons and I mentioned the request to Arnaldo Coelho. Five minutes later he returned with a beautifully woven CBD badge. The Brazilian

FA secretary, their equivalent to Ted Croker, had actually unpicked the stitching round the badge of the blazer he was wearing and presented it as a souvenir. 'Mr Patrick, for you it is no problem at all,' Coelho assured me.

Argentina, thanks a lot.

9   Assessing the situation

T he use of assessors by the Football League to check the
way in which matches are being controlled has been
attacked by both clubs and referees. The assessors have
been sinisterly described as 'League spies' and the thought
that Big Brother is watching you up in the stand certainly
unnerves some men with the whistle.

For my part I am one hundred per cent behind the scheme
in general though I feel that certain aspects of it must be
overhauled and modernised. The system used by UEFA is,
to my way of thinking, much more acceptable and constructive.

However I did more than most to assure the re-
tention of assessors during my time as president of the
Association of Football League Referees and Linesmen when
there was a concerted effort by club managers to have them
scrapped.

The scheme was widely launched in 1969 after a two-year
pilot project and means every referee and every linesman
has his performance checked in every game. League assessors
are all former referees or linesmen who have experienced
the game at its highest level. They arrive at the ground
unannounced and incognito, sit in the stand, and analyse
what they have seen from a purely technical point of view.
A detailed six-part report, awarding an overall mark out
of ten, is submitted to the League and a duplicate without

the mark and the name of the assessor is passed on to the referee.

The objections are obvious. Some referees don't like someone sitting in judgement on them though in the main they are referees whose control leaves something to be desired, and the clubs feel the power has been taken away from them.

Prior to the adoption of the assessors scheme the only marking of a referee was from the two clubs and it was on that average over a season that refs could be taken off the League list. Clubs still submit their report but now a referee has the added safeguard of an extra set of marks to help protect his career.

The opposition to assessors probably reached its peak in 1975 when I sat on a Committee of Study looking into the wide aspects of improving the game. The Secretaries and Managers Association demanded that assessors should be sacked and the basis of the argument put forward by Don Revie and Ron Greenwood was that referees adopted the attitude: 'We must do it – the bloke up there is watching.' As our president I spoke at some length in favour of assessors pointing out that it was far better for someone who had been actively involved in carrying out the laws of the game to judge a performance. The clubs, while wholly professional, were always likely to be coloured by a result in their assessment of a referee. It was also my belief that the reports, with one or two outstanding exceptions, had been of great benefit to me.

Where I think the scheme could be improved is in doing away with all the secrecy which inevitably leads to suspicion. As I have already stated assessors remain anonymous. They are not encouraged by the Football League to mix with us in any way at the game and their signature is deliberately left off the duplicate of their report which is forwarded to the referee. The reasoning is that any contact could lead to argument and that it is irrelevant who is giving the criticism or advice.

Maybe that is so – I know of referees who can't express themselves on match decisions without blowing their tops – but in the main more would be gained by adopting the European method.

UEFA not only encourage fraternisation they demand it. The assessor approaches the referee and linesmen in the dressing-room prior to a game and discusses general topics then returns on the final whistle for a further consultation before submitting his report. He'll even pay a visit at half-time if he feels a particular point needs clarification.

Surely that is much better than the farce of what happened at a Huddersfield–Blackpool match. I was relaxing in my car outside the ground as normal when I saw another car drive past. 'Hey, that's so-and-so,' I said to my wife. 'I'll just have a quick word.' As I went to say hello he accelerated to the far end of the car park, turned his back, and ducked hurriedly behind a wall to avoid me. That was my assessor for the day, a former colleague scared to say a couple of words of greeting.

Some referees actually seek out the club secretaries in an effort to discover who the assessor is. It's all so silly – as often as not their writing and phrasing on the report gives them away.

The UEFA method of consultation would have avoided one particular set of correspondence which arose from the Leeds United v Liverpool match at Elland Road in October, 1977. I was accused of letting down a colleague by the assessor when in fact I was the one let down but total lack of contact between assessor and referee meant he wasn't aware of what really had happened.

In his report he wrote: 'The game was well controlled

and I believe that the fact that not one free-kick had to be awarded until the sixteenth minute also showed that the players gave you their full respect realising that any misdemeanours would be sharply dealt with. Bearing this in mind I was rather surprised that you did not have words with the home No 6 in the 79th minute when he followed through with a tackle using his feet and elbow to bring down an opponent after the ball had gone. This was brought to your attention by Mr Waters, your linesman, and I felt that this was a let down of your colleague when you neither had words with the offender or awarded a free-kick to the other side. I thought that this was the only flaw in an otherwise excellent performance.'

What happened on the field was vastly different from what the assessor thought he saw from the stand. Phil Waters was flagging, a player was down, and looked to be in need of attention which he then received. I walked towards Phil on the line and said: 'Which player was it and do I send him off or caution him?' to which Phil replied: 'You'll never believe this, Pat, but I'm not certain. It could have been one of three players.' Afterwards he repeated what he had told me on the field and apologised for letting me down.

Actions without the help of words can be deceiving especially viewed from a distance – how often do fans see things wrongly? Of course the assessor was sincere in his remarks but surely this is the strongest possible reason for official liaison to eliminate such mistakes. A short chat with Phil and I in the dressing-room would have cleared up any misunderstanding. As it was I was duty bound to inform the League of the true facts and the assessor promptly said how sorry he was.

A lot of referees won't go back to the League for clarification of comments though Lytham St Annes are keen for the facility to be used. Assessors themselves, I maintain, want to work with us as was evident in October of 1971 when I was picked up in the official report of a Manchester United–Derby County match at Old Trafford for what was described as 'a violent foul' by Denis Law which went unpunished. The word violent, indeed the whole incident, concerned me because I was unable to recall it readily and I asked the League if they would approach the assessor for more details.

Back came the answer with the preface: 'It is refreshing to me to hear of a referee who is so interested in perfecting his performance and I am delighted to provide the necessary information.'

That is an example of the assessors scheme at its best with co-operation and courtesy on both sides. I didn't agree even after further graphic information that Law's tackle was anything like violent but I appreciated another professional's point of view and how he came to it. What does untold harm are the few faceless people who feel they must justify their existence by long-winded reports punctuated by facetious comments and laced with sarcasm.

As I say fortunately they are few and far between but they exist and I fell foul of one of the worst in October, 1976 when I became involved in my biggest wrangle with correspondence between the assessor, the Football League and myself spread over three months.

The match was York City v Northampton and the report, typed without spacing between the lines to cram as much in as possible, included the following:

Application of Laws and Control: In the last fifteen minutes we were treated to antics by one home player which should have resulted in far stricter disciplinary action than that imposed. After his first scything tackle which fortunately failed to make contact with the Northampton winger who was in full flight you had a brief word with the offender. Subsequently he repeated his action within a matter of minutes on another opponent in the same crude manner, on this occasion completing the challenge. This time you deemed it worthy to not even speak to him but simply awarded the requisite free-kick. Finally, almost as the ninety minutes expired he ran towards a visiting player, advertised his intentions to everyone, and then proceeded to put his intentions into effect.

The final whistle went immediately with no visible action taken against this man and I was left wondering just how far he would have gone before you would have decided enough was enough. Had all this occurred in the earlier stages with the same minimum amount of control I feel you would have made a major contribution towards the retaliatory action which would have been forthcoming from the visitors.

Positioning and Fitness: In common with many Football League referees you adopt an indifferent attitude towards the place kick supervising it from some fancy fifteen yards distance. When the second Northampton goal was scored the York goalkeeper had rushed from his goal and, well outside the penalty area, had parried a shot with his hands. No decision was given and the ball rebounded to the attacker who then scored – a fortuitous coincidence for yourself and your linesman or a marvellous play-on?

Stoppages and Signals: The ceremonial free-kick whilst not causing the problems of a couple of seasons ago still irritatingly holds up play. Gaining of ground at both free-kicks and throw-ins sensibly checked.

From a refereeing viewpoint that assessment, and I use the word loosely, was like a red rag to a bull.

1. The assessor was suggesting on the 'evidence' of a few

minutes that the referee was never in complete control throughout the game.

2. He committed the cardinal sin for an assessor of not dealing in facts but surmising what could have happened with sinister suggestions of retaliation which never took place. He also indulged in hypothetical questions wondering when I would have decided 'enough was enough.'

3. Accused the referee of an indifferent attitude to place kicks supervising them from 'some fancy fifteen yards distance.' What on earth is that?

4. Sarcastic comments . . . 'fortuitous coincidence or marvellous play-on?' If he didn't know why did he comment?

5. He complained of 'ceremonial free-kicks' holding up play yet in the next breath contradicted himself by saying the gaining of ground was sensibly checked.

No, this man had appointed himself God sitting on high above the ref and had indulged in everything but what the scheme was designed for – constructive criticism aimed at helping a referee improve his standards. Sarcasm and assumptions we don't want, or expect, from our former colleagues.

I took great exception to his attitude and just as he picked holes in my performance I systematically picked holes in his in my reply to the League. He had even finished with the sentence: 'Played in a sparsely filled ground, very little generated public support, fine evening, damp atmosphere, good stud hold.' What verbal diarrhoea. What trivia.

The intriguing thing was his second letter via Lytham. While it produced no further constructive comment, rather a hasty and totally unsatisfactory defence of his own stand, it was couched in a very different style and grammar formation. In short I believe the assessor did not submit the second report but got someone else to do so for him – an opinion which was shared by another assessor to whom I showed the two sets of correspondence.

Once again I challenged the conclusions and the League eventually requested that we call it a draw. What would be a step in the right direction is if the League appointed someone to assess the assessors – to check their reports for facetious or offensive remarks and erase them thereby creating a better feeling between assessor and referee.

If comments are deserved or constructive I have always been able to accept them in the right manner without squealing. Here are a couple of examples of assessors railroading me when I held up my hands:

Derby County v Everton (September 1973): You are surely aware that offences are not reduced by players making apologetic gestures at each other. There was a disturbing incident in the second-half of offences involving holding, pushing and tripping. Some of these offences, blind side to you, were not picked up by your linesman. Advice? Don't be hoodwinked by the apologies and increase your awareness of offence situations.

Arsenal v Birmingham City (October 1973): I was disturbed by your nonchalant manner and complete disregard of the fact that players of both sides questioned and at times openly showed dissent against your decisions and yet you never took any action against any player for so doing. It was fortunate that the final decision of the game had no bearing on the result as you certainly failed to carry out the law on this occasion i.e. the infringement of the penalty area by defending players at the taking of a penalty kick.

I was hit hard on both occasions but I knew I'd had a bad game and while it didn't make pleasant reading it was justified.

At one stage the Football League stopped sending copies of assessors' reports to referees because a few refs couldn't take the sort of criticism I've just outlined. A number of us hit the roof pointing out in the strongest possible terms that the effectiveness of the assessments was virtually nil if we weren't aware of the contents. Normal service was then resumed.

Just in case you are wondering how on earth I have escaped being slung off the League list after all the reports I have quoted let me modestly point out that quite a few have been glowing. One in particular was short and sweet and gave me a good chuckle. It was on the Blackburn Rovers–Bolton Wanderers match in April, 1978 and under each heading such as application of laws and control, positioning and fitness, advantage, stoppages and signals etc was one word: excellent. Finally, under general remarks and summing up, he wrote: 'Excellent. This must be my briefest report.'

Some time later I met the man I believed had the limited vocabulary and said: 'Hey, I've a complaint about you – you can't spell excellent.' He gawped and replied: 'Blimey, did I get it wrong?'

'Ah,' I said, 'It was your report then!'

The best assessor the Football League has is my wife Margaret. Before the advent of the assessment scheme she would ask me why I did this or that during a game and, as with most husbands challenged by their wife about work, I always replied to the effect that she knew little about the subject anyway. Two years later official assessors were asking the same questions.

One of our dear friends, John Thacker, always used to relate a story about how Margaret made him sit up and think about his refereeing. He was officiating at Middlesbrough and called at our house after the game. John asked what I thought of his performance and Margaret broke in to say: 'You know what's wrong John? You lack one thing –

you haven't the bastard instinct. You're too nice to people.'
She was spot on. There must be a certain ruthlessness in a
referee's make-up and John lacked it. He was a great bloke
and his death a little while back was a sad blow to us all.

The assessment scheme has survived a rough ride but
three other Football League and FA ideas have not. I
mourn the passing of one; applaud the passing of the other
two.

The pre-match talks with players had so much to recommend it yet it ran for only about three seasons after its
inception late in 1969. The trouble was the same as that
which we would face if we accepted the UEFA style of
assessing . . . some of us cannot handle ourselves in open
discussion.

Originally the turning of the key to previously forbidden
territory for referees was heralded with a fanfare of trum-
pets by the clubs. A better, firmer understanding between
players and referees was foreseen. My first game under the
new League experiment was Manchester United–Spurs at
Old Trafford before 53, 000 fans, a match Manchester United
won 3–1 with two stunning goals by Bobby Charlton. I
had never been able to relax at Old Trafford on previous
visits but the dressing-room chats seemed to work wonders
in making for an easy atmosphere.

The old thorny question of free-kicks provided most of
the discussion with one or two players asking questions on
interpretation. I stressed that I would allow free-kicks to be
taken quickly only if they were in the half of the field being
defended by the team awarded them and warned that the
ten-yard rule would be rigidly enforced. On swearing I
underlined I would stand no abuse to officials or other
players.

Thus all misunderstanding was cleared up in advance,
which I've maintained was the great strength of the scheme,

and the game went like a dream. Matt Busby, highly com-
plimentary afterwards, said: 'It was a good, honest discussion and it unquestionably helped keep the game flowing
more smoothly than in the past.'

Later I made Italian history by giving a pre-match talk
to the Torino players before their Anglo-Italian League Cup-
winners' Cup tie with Spurs in the Luigi Ferraris Stadium.
Their coach Gustavo Giagnoni was so impressed that he
advocated it for all future European competitions stating:
'My players were able to know how the referee would
interpret the laws and it greatly helped the match to be
such a sporting one.' Praise indeed, especially as the Italians
had lost at home 1–0!

However all the great expectations fizzled out and finally
died and I lay the blame firmly at the door of the referees.
It was a case of a few spoiling it for many.

Some refs began saying they would do this, that and the
other and then didn't when it came to the crunch. Others
wanted to be one of the boys and began cracking jokes in
the dressing-room. One, who shall remain nameless, even
boasted: 'I'm a bastard out there so I'm going to be a
bastard in here as well.' Clubs began to complain, rightly
so, and a scheme so full of potential was stopped.

The old disciplinary hearings also went the journey but
that was good riddance. The clubs dreadfully misused the
system which became farcical. They would appeal against
a caution purely to make the offender available for an
important game coming up while a personal hearing was
arranged. Though the FA tried not to inconvenience the
referee we were travelling the length and breadth of the
country and some of the things which went on in the
meetings were unbelievable.

One of the daftest was when Larry Lloyd, then with
Liverpool, appealed against a caution and we all trudged off

to Lancaster Gate for the hearing. We went through all
the verbals and then Liverpool called TV evidence. Telly is
an angle of deception to start with and I was getting pretty
cheesed off by now but that was nothing to what was to
come. The chairman of the committee, a most respected
name in football, finally asked the rest of the commission
if they would like to see the film backwards and we all sat
there like a bunch of morons as this thing was played
through the wrong way – twice!

We were then asked if we would adjourn to an ante
room while the commission deliberated their findings and I
said to Larry: 'After that little lot you're certain to get off.'
He laughed and said: 'I'll give you a hundred pounds if I
do.' I'm still waiting for the cheque.

On another occasion a Carlisle player, Les O'Neill, arrived
with a director to contest a caution he received against
Sunderland only to find a Sunderland director, Syd Collings,
sitting in judgement. Mr Collings duly stepped down to
avoid embarrassment but what then occurred showed me
how devious clubs can be.

Carlisle's case was that I had said 'sorry' to O'Neill for
cautioning him when, in fact, what I had said was: 'I'm
sorry about this, Les, but he left you with no option, did
he?' after the player had brought down an opponent. The
word 'sorry' had been cleverly taken out of context and
used to try and manufacture an escape route. O'Neill was
found guilty and the caution recorded but I learned one
major thing from that incident and that was never to
sympathise with players.

Referees used to go round saying they had 'won' or
'lost' a case which always made me mad. Cases were
never won or lost. A referee did his job on the field of play
in either cautioning or sending off a player (we caution
people – showbusiness agents book them) and he didn't

need a commission to tell him whether he had done it properly or not.

Another scheme to bite the dust is one which is still periodically given a revival by First Division managers and that's to have our so-called top referees exclusively handle all the top games.

The Football League tried it a few years ago selecting around eighteen refs to take charge of crucial First and Second Division matches and derbies in the Third and Fourth Divisions but familiarity breeds contempt and a ref handling, say Liverpool or Manchester United, four or five times in a matter of weeks was far from satisfactory.

I'm staunchly against the formation of a select band of referees be it at the request of the clubs or otherwise. There are ninety-two clubs in the Football League and when we are invited to become part of the system we must be prepared to go to any club. I know some referees think they are too big to handle certain matches – I've come across some who have not been 'available' when an FA Youth Cup game has come up. Others say they can't produce their best in the lower divisions. Gordon Hill was one of these people. He stated he needed the big-match atmosphere. A current FIFA referee apparently suffers from the same allergy according to a Fourth Division club I visited in his wake who told me this particular ref seemed disinterested.

That to me is a terrible condemnation of a referee. Perhaps I'm lucky but I don't have to be on a stage with a 60,000 audience to enjoy a match. I can get the same self satisfaction padding round a local ground.

Last season I did the Halifax–Reading match in the Fourth Division and the local radio kept prattling on about one of the biggest names in football being here – me. Okay, that's nice but what was even nicer was that I enjoyed the game. Most of the smaller clubs are so friendly, so welcoming that it is a joy to go there.

My affection for Barrow, for example, was special. I took my first Football League game at Holker Street and my first FA Cup tie and I was genuinely upset when they were voted out of the League. They still live in my memory.

10   Bribery

No one has ever proved that an English referee has taken a bribe. There has never been so much as a whisper that any Football League referee has accepted money to influence the result of a game. That record of honesty is one of which we can be enormously proud.

Even during the great bribery scandals of the early 1960s when England international footballers who were household names were found guilty of throwing matches, sentenced to jail and barred sine die from the game, referees remained untainted.

The net, cast by the pools investigators, the Football League and the Sunday People newspaper, caught fish big and small; some even survived by the skin of their teeth to continue in the game. Their names are known and on file at Lytham St Annes. But there wasn't a whiff of notoriety attached to a solitary referee, the one person above all who would appear a ready target for the fixers.

While I will not pretend we have cornered the market in honest men there is no question that the integrity of the English referee is respected world wide.

Not so many years ago Greece used to import English refs like Ken Dagnall to handle their important domestic cup games because of the need for absolute impartiality. They felt they could not guarantee it from within their own boundaries. Italy is another country which has been rocked by bribery scandals with referees allegedly coming by lucrative summer holidays at the expense of certain clubs.

Let me state from the outset that I have never been offered a bribe. Needless to say had I been I would have reported it without hesitation – my career, my pride and my sense of decency are worth more than money can buy.

However refereeing abroad can be full of unseen pitfalls for the naïve. The biggest is the presentation of gifts, not cash, and it is in this grey area where doubt can be cast.

In the last year Scotland's top referee John Gordon and his two linesmen were suspended for three years for allegedly accepting exorbitant gifts from AC Milan before officiating in one of their European matches. The ban has effectively finished Gordon's international career but what has disappointed and puzzled me is how a man of his experience who refereed in the World Cup finals could allow himself to get into such a position.

UEFA lay down stringent laws regarding the acceptance of gifts and, having travelled the world extensively, I am only too aware of how, with language differences to add to any misunderstanding, an innocent situation can suddenly take on sinister connotations if those guidelines are not strictly adhered to. That is why I am so firm and demanding not only of myself but my linesmen when we go abroad. It is not enough for a referee to be whiter than white. He must be seen to be whiter than white.

The UEFA ruling on hospitality is worth giving in its entirety because it is the basis upon which we must all work. It says:

Referees and linesmen must refuse firmly but politely any exaggerated and all too generous hospitality. Souvenir gifts should not be accepted before but only after the game. The acceptance of valuables is strictly prohibited; the same applies to the charging of additional daily allowances. The acceptance of other than souvenir presents or of invitations to prolong the stay in the country of the organiser is prohibited. Any attempt of influencing the referee before the match shall be reported immediately to the delegate or to the General Secretariat of UEFA. The referees and the linesmen are nominated for an impartial control of the matches and their behaviour must be accordingly. The Referees' Committee will pay particular attention to this aspect and take rigorous measures if necessary.

One of the key phrases in that document is the one which says souvenirs should not be accepted before a game. They could, of course, be interpreted as a bribe if they were.

The difficulty here is that the referee and linesmen are sometimes invited to dinner on the eve of the match by the host club, along with officials of their opponents, and the clubs want to make the presentations then – all above board but technically at the wrong time. What do you do not to snub anyone but at the same time not leave anything open to conjecture? I've come up with my own answer to that one – I accept the gift with grace but make a point of not opening it. My linesmen, previously primed, do likewise. If the UEFA observer is present, as he often is, we may actually hand over the wrapped gifts for him to keep until after the game. It's a compromise which appears to work well.

My caution goes right down the line. I've even pulled the linesmen to one side as we've left a restaurant and asked them to remove a pin badge and put it on the under side of their lapel. Small point? I think not. Imagine the ref or linesmen turning up at Old Trafford for a Manchester United–Liverpool match in front of a full house with a Liverpool badge in his jacket when his impartiality has to be unquestioned. That's what it amounts to.

Even in this country I watch the colour trap. No way will I arrive at a Liverpool–Everton derby in a blue suit and Margaret knows not to wear a red dress. Supporters we can't afford to be in anyone's eyes.

During the chat with my colleagues, usually on the plane going out, I tell them should they require anything at all would they please tell me rather than a club courier. It's not a matter of snooping, merely commonsense gathered through experience. The need to exercise restraint was simply displayed in 1970 when I officiated at the Anglo-Italian match between Napoli and Swindon in Naples. I like Italian whistles and always use one in our League matches over here. They are high pitched and can be plainly heard above the din of a match, something I first learned through watching a Continental match on television. Being in the country where they are manufactured, it was natural I should want to purchase a supply so I approached the Napoli club courier to ask where was the best place to find them. The next morning he pulled out a parcel containing three metal whistles and three plastic ones. Money was politely refused. They were a gift I was told with a smile.

In this case it didn't really matter. Whistles if not ten a penny are almost that and I gave four away as it was. But I may have been enquiring where to buy a crystal vase or an expensive piece of leather wear and suddenly found, instead of receiving directions to a shopping centre, I was knee deep in goods.

The call for full-time referees in England is one I oppose for many reasons not least because I am of the opinion bribery would become more of a threat if our livelihoods depended solely on football. Imagine a referee with only a few months to go to enforced retirement at the age of forty-seven with no recognised profession or trade to fall back

on being approached by some unscrupulous character offer-
ing him £10,000 or £20,000 in ready cash. It could just be
tempting.

I believe there isn't a referee on the Football League list
today who would contemplate such a thing but I don't know
for certain, do I? And even if in years to come only one out
of hundreds took the plunge it would be enough to destroy
all the trust, all the standing, we have painstakingly built
up over more than half a century. Better that we keep our
independence. Honest decisions are in no doubt that
way.

There would be practical difficulties in going full-time, of
course. For a start the League would probably offer no more
than a two-year contract so what happens to our members
who have good jobs – do they joyously throw away years of
hard work? There have been doctors, solicitors and bank
managers amongst us. We've even had an MP in Denis
Howell. They would hardly fall over themselves for a
guaranteed future of twenty-four months. Then there's the
question of referees kicked off the League list.

FA secretary Ted Croker is a strong advocator of full-time
referees and a couple of years ago we clashed publicly over
the issue. Mr Croker, speaking at a Sports Writers' Association luncheon in London, said that British referees were
no longer the best in the world and added: 'The rest of the
world has concentrated on training referees to a high
standard. There are lots of steps that could be taken to
improve our referees. The problem is inconsistency rather
than ability. The demands that are made are totally un-
reasonable to ask of part-time referees.'

He went on to say that he would like to see six professional referees, or a maximum of twelve, who would
officiate at fifty to sixty games a year.

Asked to respond I ventured that if we weren't the best in

the world why then was the FA getting a lot of requests to send our referees abroad to coach. As for being professional I had handled fifty-nine matches at all levels the previous season spending more time on football than on my farm. Our referees couldn't be more professional in their attitude, I maintained.

The upshot was a phone call from Mr Croker inviting me to Lancaster Gate for a chat on the subject. Basically we remained entrenched in our beliefs but there was a lot of open discussion and it was productive insofar as we had a better understanding of each other's point of view.

But full-time referees . . . the glib answer is that I haven't time to be one, I'm too busy with football. Though, come to think of it, that's not too far from the truth. With the matches themselves; North East section meetings of the Association of FLR and L, and Referees' Association coaching sessions; acting as guest speaker at referees' dinners as far afield as Rochdale, Preston and Doncaster; plus participating in fringe events such as judging beauty contests etc football dominates my life.

Okay, I'm something of a one-off. In a privileged position, if you like, since quitting industry to go into partnership with my brother-in-law on the farm which makes me my own boss with the best possible help on hand. My wife is wonderfully understanding, we have no children, and consequently I can pour so much into sport. But nevertheless the bulk of referees are committed men who willingly give up valuable time. They are hardly in it for the cash and the glory is strictly limited in relation to players or even managers.

On the other point, the physical training of referees, it is totally unnecessary to undergo daily work-outs. Referees do not kick a ball or jump for it to sap their strength and so require a limited programme to that of players. Neither will full-time training improve two of his greatest assets, his eyesight and his courage.

11   Getting together

I'm a passionate believer and campaigner for better relationships between players and referees. Since I became a
Football League referee in 1966 I have made it my business
to try and bring together our two main bodies, the
Association of Football League Referees and Linesmen and
the Professional Footballers' Association, to create genuine
respect and friendship.

Take it from me, it's not easy – for some reason it's like
trying to mix oil and water. Yet, if attitudes are constructive, it can be done. Indeed it must be done and,
happily, we are moving in the right direction even if it's at
a sedate pace rather than a gallop.

No football match, however large or small in status, can
take place without a referee and two linesmen. They are
the third team which some folk tend to overlook. In their
own way they are as important as the twenty-two players
and it is the atmosphere of trust or suspicion, respect or
cynicism, acceptance or defiance between the two bodies
which to a large degree determines the quality of entertainment served up to the spectators. Football is a game for
three teams not two.

Any bond cannot be forged solely on the field of play.
It must, to my mind, be fashioned off it. I've long maintained
the need for players and referees to mix informally away
from the public eye and I don't mean only the politicians of
our respective associations getting together though that is

essential as a basis to work on. I'm talking about football clubs inviting League refs who live in their area to visit them for midweek chats and for referees' societies to ask players along to address them. Attacking the problem at grassroots level and breaking down the barriers of 'us' and 'them.'

I've campaigned through the newspapers, through television on Match of the Day, and through more formal channels within football to stir players, clubs and referees alike but I felt my greatest opportunity to make a major breakthrough was during my time as our association president in 1975 when a Committee of Study was set up to look into all aspects of football.

Previously whenever I had brought up the subject among fellow referees there was a severe shaking of the head, a sharp intake of breath as though a cardinal sin had been suggested, and the stern assurance that the Football League would never allow it. That I couldn't believe and, once firmly ensconced in the hot seat, it seemed the perfect opportunity to take the bull by the horns and confront soccer's various leaders.

The Committee of Study comprised of representatives from the Football Association and Football League, plus managers and players, as well as referees . . . a comprehensive cross section of opinion if you like. Far from knocking the player-referee relationship authority appeared delighted with the idea. Ted Croker and Alan Hardaker were generous in their encouragement and my overall feeling was one of euphoria tinged with regret that a lot of years had been wasted. However all good things are worth waiting for and though the PFA in the form of chairman Derek Dougan were evasive and non-committal, a foretaste of things to come, it was at first sight a victory for commonsense.

Believing that good foundations are built in the North East I journeyed home to make an impression on my own doorstep. What was to happen nationally tomorrow could happen locally today. My enthusiasm obviously rubbed off on our members who agreed to invite Bob Moncur, then the area representative on the PFA executive, to address our next meeting at Roker Park. Moncur, later to become manager of Carlisle United, was a player of considerable stature having captained Sunderland, Newcastle United and Scotland and his acceptance was warmly greeted by the North East referees.

Come the meeting, however, there was no sign of Moncur and a few members were uptight about the apparent snub. The get-together was on a Sunday afternoon and only twenty-four hours earlier Moncur had been reminded of the date and time at Sunderland's match. His actions were more likely to drive a wedge between players and referees rather than cement a new band of friendship but I wasn't prepared to ditch a good idea on one setback and maintained that there could be a very good reason for a non-appearance.

The argument was accepted, albeit with reservations, and to show good faith Moncur was once again invited to address us, this time at St James's Park. Once more a letter of confirmation was sent off, phone calls were made, and he failed to appear with no explanation offered.

There's no denying that I was hurt, deeply hurt. Not because I was president of our Association and had lost face or because I was on an ego trip indulging in my pet whims but because I believed beyond question that the game of football needed much closer ties between its participants on the field of play. These two instances however unfortunate or accidental, underlined what was wrong – a total lack of communication.

The redeeming feature of all this was the attitude of another player, equally prominent within the PFA hierarchy. Third time lucky, they say. Well, it was for me when, a little later, I went further up the road to Newcastle United to personally ask Alan Gowling to pay us a visit.

All right, I was thick skinned but why not? It was worth it when Gowling actually put in an appearance. The meeting went like a bomb, plenty of healthy give-and-take with a lot of new information gleaned by both parties at the end of the day.

Big Alan pressed for more communication between us strongly advocating an after-match drink together. At such time, a player could reasonably ask a referee to explain a decision during the game, and although there was a risk of an argument, he felt much more good would come out of such face-to-face discussions. On the old question of over-the-top tackling he conceded that players have a moral obligation to put a stop to such a practice but claimed that the referee is the man who has the direct authority to clamp down by issuing marching orders for the first deliberate offence of this nature in a game – a draw, I think. And, finally, he agreed that generally speaking players don't know the laws of the game as they should. It is up to the clubs to make young footballers aware of the laws and their application and coaches should test them on their knowledge. Equally it would help if referees took the coaching certificate. As you see, interesting, honest stuff which gave us all food for thought.

Spreading the gospel among the clubs has, over the years, seen me address players' meetings at Middlesbrough, Hartlepool and Darlington. These usually take place in midweek after training though Hartlepool boss Billy Horner actually broke up a training session and brought the players off the field for our tête-à-tête. What a session that was – two hours of deep discussion with the club chairman, Vince Barker, not only present but sticking in his tuppence worth as well.

The steady progress I've talked about is best illustrated by the very significant step we all took a few months back. Twenty of our members including assessors as well as referees and linesmen met players, managers, and coaches from Boro, Newcastle United, Sunderland, Hartlepool and Darlington at Ayresome Park to exchange views. A real feather in everyone's cap – especially as the talk-in was totally secret and never leaked out in the Press either beforehand or afterwards. Even the most cynical could hardly call it a publicity stunt, could they?

Boro, as I've explained, are a special case. I used to live on the same estate as a lot of their players and I pop down to Ayresome Park regularly for treatment or whatever. Often I'll sit round the dressing-room or the shower room having a natter with a player and while I realise the bond that has grown up is somewhat out of the ordinary and unlikely to be repeated nationally there is no reason not to aim for utopia. John Hickton is an example of the deep friendship fostered with the aid of time. I ordered him off in a pre-season friendly at Ayresome yet he still asked me to ref his testimonial match.

Manager John Neal has invited many of our local referees to either train with the Boro or actually handle five-a-side matches and it's the latter which excites me. Our younger, more inexperienced members should not hesitate to take advantage of such generosity if only to witness the competitive spirit which abounds even in training.

I've seen players in a five-a-side on the car park argue vehemently with the coach over a decision which has gone against them. Now, a lot of our members can't accept that feelings get so heated in training as to produce such a scene yet it's perfectly true. Clubs build competitive qualities into a player.

There is a very thin line between appeal and dissent and

what we have to learn is to know what to accept and when a player wants to take you to the cleaners. If you can't sort out that then you may as well be sitting in the stand barracking the ref for the good you're doing on the field.

What I would also advocate is for referees to go onto sports panels with players. Never mind the drag on time or availability, a few moments over a quiet drink afterwards can be the equivalent of years of a quick 'hello' outside a football ground on a Saturday afternoon.

To players we are like policemen – figures which must be given respect, outwardly at least, but always likely to nick you if you aren't careful. The finger of suspicion is on both sides, of course, and it's no good me saying that the player and referee is equal the whole of the time. That can't be so. For ninety minutes the referee is the representative of the Football Association and as such must adjudicate fairly and without favour. There will always be a difference but it should be minimal.

The crusader in me goes beyond players and referees and envelops the supporters as well. With so much violence on the terraces due, in part, to ignorance I would like to see Supporters' Clubs invite referees to their meetings to discuss the laws. This would help supporters to be more conversant with the laws and help them understand the match officials' interpretation of them during actual games.

While the North East has done its small share, nationally the theme of comradeship hasn't been developed to quite the same degree. During Derek Dougan's spell as chairman of the PFA he showed a disappointing indifference to the problem which I could never understand. The PFA can't be asked to carry the can alone, however. With little response coming from the other side we should have hammered it more ourselves. Optimism has increased with Gordon Taylor at the helm and, backed by a good executive and the hard-working Cliff Lloyd, the PFA and the Association of Football League Referees and Linesmen could be heading towards the same wavelength. A good sign was that for the first time ever the PFA was due to address our conference this year.

We've had the likes of Brian Clough speaking (he got a standing ovation two years ago for a no-punches-pulled speech) and PFA officials have always been at our banquet but, until now, they have never taken the floor at conference.

At the beginning of the chapter I referred to three teams taking part in a football match and the regulations governing that third team have changed in one significant aspect in recent times.

When I joined the Football League fourteen years ago it was stipulated that the referee and linesmen should report to the ground at least forty-five minutes before the kick-off. It didn't take me long to realise that this was totally inadequate. Some people take three quarters of an hour to get changed and with the interruption of the managers handing in the team sheets thirty minutes before the off the time for a three-way talk was negligible. On several occasions a referee may not know one of his linesmen personally yet he was expected to form a tangible understanding inside forty-five minutes and go out there onto the park as one unit.

Make no mistake, the understanding of the third team is of paramount importance. If they don't help each other no one else will help them and if they get it wrong everyone else will suffer.

Some of us kicked up a bit of dust over that forty-five minute rule on the grounds that we needed more time for our own team-talk and preparation. Fortunately we were listened to and now it's an hour and a half deadline. I

consider the ninety minutes before a game of equal importance to the ninety minutes which follow.

To the outsider it must look as though we have two
conflicting unions – the Association of Football League
Referees and Linesmen and the Referees' Association. That
is not so. In reality they are complementary to each other
and I am a great believer in both. I only wish some other
referees were.

The Referees' Association is for us all. The moment you
pass your first exam you can join and I've been a member
for twenty-six years. Its aims are to improve the standard
of refereeing, to promote closer relationships between
referees and the governing bodies and to assist referees'
societies in their educational work.

The Association of FLR and L is geared solely to co-ordin-
ating the needs of members for one competition and that is
the Football League.

Sadly some referees opt out of the RA once they make the
League list and others don't even join in the first place.
What I would like to see is it made compulsory for all
referees to be members of the Referees' Association. Force
them to learn if they won't do so voluntarily. The RA helps
a young referee by allowing him to make his mistakes in
the meeting room rather than on the field with a wealth of
experience on tap to dig him out. Certainly I owe them
a debt of gratitude for helping me along the road and
in particular I owe one to Arnold Ward, a former vice-
president.

Arnold was a gem. He lived in Middlesbrough and if ever
I had a mental blockage when working on my report I'd give
him a ring and he'd hop on his bike (he didn't have a car)
and pedal furiously over to our house to give me the
benefit of his expert knowledge. Arnold typified the
Referees' Association motto 'Service before Self' always

being ready to give advice if requested but never willing to boost an already inflated ego.

He was a natural coach and tutor who eventually found his niche in life after rising no higher than the Football League line in his active days. His expertise was such that he was known as one of the three wise men on the laws of the game. It was a tragedy that Arnold died prior to my FA Cup final. To him seeing one of his proteges at Wembley would have been better than being there himself.

The strides made by the RA are best illustrated by the fact that we have acquired a full-time secretary, Owen Venning, in the last couple of years. The appointment of a competent administrator to the payroll to work alongside honorary president Ken Burns has meant us becoming more professional in our outlook.

To the best of my knowledge only one person has ever had his membership of the Association of Football League Referees and Linesmen withdrawn. Unfortunately it happened during my term as president and, with hindsight, I bitterly regret the action we took.

That person was Ricky Nicholson and it occurred because of his public criticism of Clive Thomas's handling of a match.

Ricky was quite an extrovert character. A successful businessman who drove round in a Rolls, he wore a toupee and one day at Newcastle it blew off as he was running towards the Leazes end. Without breaking stride he caught the wig one-handed in mid-air and stuffed it into his pocket. Most of the crowd missed the split second action. To them the ref had a full head of hair one minute and was as bald as a coot the next. The ground buzzed with conversation for the rest of the match. A hair-raising experience, certainly, but the story goes that the astute Ricky got two expensive hair pieces free of charge from the makers because they were guaranteed not to move.

After he had retired from refereeing Ricky wrote the occasional article for a newspaper and the storm blew up when he really hammered Clive Thomas over his performance in a particular game. Ricky was called before the Association and, after a full hearing, was asked to give an undertaking that he would never repeat such actions. He said he couldn't do that – he had voiced an honest opinion. We felt obliged under the circumstances to withdraw his membership.

In other words we backed Clive and dismissed a colleague in his defence, a colleague who had been secretary of the Association at one time. Yet Clive was later quoted in a newspaper as saying that Association meetings were a waste of time because they didn't discuss football and he declined to speak at our conference on his return from Argentina.

The whole affair of Ricky Nicholson and Clive Thomas leaves me rather disgusted.

Neither the Referees' Association nor the Association of Football League Referees and Linesmen is a union in the strictest sense of the word and I pray they never will be. Don't misunderstand me, I'm all in favour of trade unions – I was a shop steward once – but I don't want us to become militant because we don't have to be referees. It isn't our full-time job.

Unions are there to protect men and women who have to earn a living from what they do. The idea of referees going on strike in this country is abhorrent to anyone who takes the RA motto 'Service before Self' at all seriously though I must admit that I ended up at the centre of a referees' strike when I was in Kuwait. But that's another story. . . .

12   Controversy

If you can't stand the heat get out of the kitchen. That's
something I've always maintained and I've said it more
than once to aspiring (and perspiring) referees.

The kitchen can be hot, make no mistake about that. But
then it's our duty to handle such situations without the aid
of an asbestos suit and to sleep soundly that night knowing
that at least honesty has prevailed.

Certainly I slept peacefully in my bed the night of my
so-called 'trial by television' – the 1978 League Cup final
replay between Nottingham Forest and Liverpool at Old
Trafford. The world and his wife seemed caught up in the
furore of was-it-or-wasn't-it a penalty? Television dissected
the incident as clinically as any surgeon surrounding it with
emotive words which stoked the fire and topping it with
an interview which led to the player concerned, Liverpool's
central defender Phil Thompson being charged by the FA
with bringing the game into disrepute.

The whole business had been sparked off by my penalty
award which, converted by John Robertson, was to separate
these two fine sides at the end of three-and-a-half hours of
football and see the underdogs, Forest, lift the trophy.
Ready-made stuff for controversy, and eagerly gobbled up
by the media.

But for a much clearer overall picture of the League Cup
final drama we need to go back to the first game at Wembley
itself.

Liverpool, current European champions, took on the pre-
tenders to their throne Nottingham Forest who were shorn
of the talents of Peter Shilton, Archie Gemmill, Dave
Needham and Colin Barrett. Consequently the scribes had
it figured only one way – the huge, red steamroller of Liverpool would inevitably engulf and then crush brittle Forest.
It was only a matter of time.

It looked that way, too, as Liverpool attacked like fury
throughout. But these games have a habit of throwing up an
unexpected hero and so it was this time. Shilton is rated
one of the world's greatest keepers and perhaps the biggest
single influence on the Forest side but he was out cup-tied
and a big, blond 18-year-old lad called Chris Woods, who
had never played a first-team game, was thrown in as his
deputy. Woods was to carry the extra burden of being the
youngest ever keeper to play in a Wembley cup final but
he wore it like a badge of honour rather than a millstone
as he turned in a superlative performance.

As the second-half wore on with the deadlock still not
broken I said to Jimmy Case: 'Hey, what's happening here?'
He winked and replied: 'It's just a matter of time, Pat.
We're going to win this one.' If the dam had been breached
once it might have brought a flood of goals but as it was
the match stretched into extra time and tired limbs took
their toll.

After the game the topic of conversation with my two
linesmen, Charlie Cottam and Brian Robinson, was how such
a game could possibly end 0–0. Liverpool felt they had
established their superiority and when John McGovern was
added to the long list of Forest stars missing for the replay
four days later the belief that this time it was Liverpool's
pot was intensified everywhere but on the banks of the
Trent.

Wembley had left no loose ends for us to tidy up second

time around. The game had been enjoyable without ven-
dettas and the three of us went back into the game antici-
pating a cracker.

Though the penalty became the major issue, Liverpool's
frustration at being unable to turn territorial advantage into
goals was mirrored by their involvement in two other
moments of controversy in the match. The first, and most
minor, was the cautioning of Ian Callaghan just before the
interval. Cally is one of football's gentlemen and a referee
taking his name is, in some eyes, little short of committing
treason.

It was widely reported that this was the first time in 849
matches the Callaghan had been cautioned which, in fact,
wasn't true. He had received a similiar caution in a friendly
four years earlier but it hadn't been recorded.

In an eight-minute spell I had to show the yellow card to
three players. Peter Withe and Viv Anderson were first
and second, then came Cally. There was no question that
Ian deliberately obstructed his opponent . . . he ran two
steps and body-checked Withe after the big forward had
played the ball past him.

A cautionable offence, no sweat, and with anyone else
involved it wouldn't have raised an eyebrow but, having
said that, let me add the rider that I'm a great admirer of
the little fellow. If all pro's had his attitude to the game it
would be very simple to handle.

The penalty came in fifty-four minutes and I saw it this
way : a quick through ball was played by Tony Woodcock
which caught the Liverpool defence square and wide to
the world. John O'Hare, sub at Wembley and playing for the
injured McGovern, was after it and accelerating into the
penalty area with Ray Clemence realising the sudden danger.
I was about nine or ten yards behind play and my view was
unrestricted as Phil Thompson came in for a last-ditch

tackle. Down went O'Hare and I knew instinctively it was
a penalty. I was convinced it was inside the area but I
glanced towards my linesman, Charlie Cottam, for confirmation. Charlie was standing there bang in line with
play, his flag firmly across his chest. That was enough ... I
pointed to the spot.

Looking back I can't honestly say I recall my parentage
being disputed by the crowd over my decision. Liverpool
chuntered in protest but there was no mass appeal of any
hostile nature. I was never subjected to jostling or shirt-
pulling. Thompson, to his credit, said nothing untoward at
this stage. Or if he did it certainly wasn't in my hearing.
Robertson stuck the penalty kick between Ray Clemence
and the right-hand post and that was it.

To me the penalty award was the result of team work
between referee and linesman and so it was with the third
controversial incident four minutes later when Liverpool
thought they had equalised. As soon as Kenny Dalglish
squared the ball to Terry McDermott the flag of Brian
Robinson was raised to signal that McDermott had controlled the ball with his upper arm and the whistle had gone
before he went on to beat Woods.

When I walked off Old Trafford with the scoreline 1–0
I had no idea that I was walking into a storm. I'd done my
job with honesty and to the best of my ability and nothing
at that stage had suggested a backlash. To the contrary, I
thought the game had been a fine one and courage had been
shown in the handling of it.

But before I'd started to get changed in the dressing-room
the TV boys were knocking at my door. There had been
some controversy and would I go on telly and be inter-
viewed to clear it up? Certainly I would.

It's always been my policy to clear up any doubts over
decisions rather than leave them to fester and grow into

even bigger issues. Besides, whatever I may be I'm not a coward and I had nothing to hide. So the interview went ahead and, without emotion, I explained my side of the story. At no time was I shown a slow motion replay of the penalty incident or was I aware of what Phil Thompson had said in his interview. In fact to this day I have never seen a film of either the Wembley final or the replay. They might make interesting viewing . . .

The TV playback was supposed to prove that O'Hare was brought down just outside the area rather than in it and Thompson told millions on television: 'It was bloody disgraceful. I admit I committed a professional foul but I was outside the area when I kicked him. That sounds bad but that's the way it was.' He added that the linesman hadn't wanted to know and had stood there with his flag across his chest. Interesting!

Let's deal with the position of contact in relation to the eighteen-yard line. TV is an angle of deception and I'm not willing to accept everything seen from a camera perched a few hundred yards away as gospel. I was a darned sight closer and to me O'Hare was inside. To a linesman of some considerable experience who was better placed he was inside, too.

While I agree that referees are only human and can make mistakes as much as the next man, I found the immediate reaction of the journalists to the same incident more than illuminating.

At night matches finishing around ten past nine journalists usually have to file a match report to their head office on the final whistle to catch the early editions. Then, with time to collect their thoughts and do a little checking, they file a rewrite for the main run of the newspaper. The first editions the following morning carried straight match reports recording the penalty without controversy but the 'city runs' were full of drama and accusations. See what I'm getting at? The naked eye had accepted without quibble that O'Hare was inside the penalty area but with the benefit of the TV slow motion seen later, and the sniff of a juicy story to serve up, opinions changed radically.

I wonder how often in the old days, before the advent of the TV slow motion re-run, borderline cases were readily accepted and equally readily forgotten about!

Phil Thompson's outburst was easy to pick holes in. To begin with he condemned himself by stating that he kicked O'Hare to the ground. I thought he merely tackled him so perhaps I was wrong twice. A professional foul deserves a professional caution.

The bit about the linesman opting out only showed that even top footballers aren't fully conversant with the laws of the game. Far from chickening out Charlie Cottam showed a good deal of courage by immediately giving me the signal I required. A flag across the chest means the act took place inside the penalty area, no such flag indicates that it was outside. It is then up to the referee to award a penalty kick or otherwise.

Obviously Thompson didn't realise that and neither did former Liverpool and Scotland centre-forward Ian St John. During the television inquest St John said I'd claimed the decision was confirmed 'but he didn't say who confirmed it,' he added with a smile.

May I recommend to Phil, Ian and many more players that they read a book entitled 'Referees' Chart and Players' Guide to the Laws of the Game.' Honestly, it's amazing how many top footballers only have a layman's knowledge of the laws and it can lead to unnecessary areas of dispute.

Whenever players take their FA coaching badge the biggest ratio of failures is over the laws of the game. I well remember going to Wilf Mannion's house long after he retired to help him prepare for a coaching exam. Here was a man I had idolised, one of the greatest players ever to pull on the white shirt of England, yet on the laws he was all awash. During one session Wilf, always an honest bloke, sat back in his chair, shook his head, and said : 'Pat, I never knew that in all the years I was playing!'

Phil's interview resulted in him being fined £300 by the FA for bringing the game into disrepute and Liverpool manager Bob Paisley banning his players from after-match telly sessions for fear of what they might say in the heat of the moment. There's no question that Phil was badly advised to sound off like that but I felt sorrow more than anger because he's basically a nice enough lad.

Trial by TV is wrong but that's not to say controversial incidents should not be shown. Far from it – this game of ours would die without controversy. If there were never any talking points for the man in the pub on a Saturday night or Sunday lunchtime the interest would quickly evaporate.

I'm not suggesting we should go looking for controversy though I know of certain referees who do. It's just that when by the very nature of the game it happens it's not necessarily a bad thing.

All referees are egotistical, it's part of our make-up, and if we love praise then we must accept criticism at times as well. Where television can be unfair is in the spoken word which goes with the picture. As often as not the commentator is not fully aware of what he's talking about yet he blithely prattles on convincing viewers of things which are wrong. Here I much prefer the radio commentators to the telly boys. They deal in fact rather than opinion.

It would help if the TV commentator had a better all-round soccer education and this is where I must hand a bouquet to Brian Moore of ITV. Brian, a director at Gilling-

ham, took a referee's examination to improve his understanding of the game.

TV has a great responsibility with its massive audience
and, thankfully, it has climbed down off its hanging stage
recently.

Last year's League Cup final wasn't the first television
crucifixion I'd been involved in. Six years earlier, in January
of 1972, Jimmy Hill had seen fit to do a job on me after the
Stoke City–West Ham League Cup semi-final, again at Old
Trafford.

It was the fourth meeting between the two teams which
had been locked together for five and a half hours and Stoke
edged it 3–2 to claim their Wembley appearance and
eventually a major trophy for the first time in 109 years.

Hill stitched me up on ITV's programme 'On the Ball'
because he alleged that a Stoke City player, John Ritchie,
was offside when Terry Conroy struck the winning goal
and that I had failed to award West Ham a penalty but
had given one to Stoke. His accusations were to have far
reaching effects with the Football League stepping in to have
the final word.

All four matches were classics in their own right. In the
first leg of the semi-final at Stoke, West Ham came from
behind to win 2–1. At Upton Park a Ritchie goal levelled
matters on aggregate but the odds were stacked heavily in
West Ham's favour when they were awarded a penalty in
the closing minutes. Gordon Banks' save from Geoff Hurst
was probably the save of the season, a superb reflex effort
which, in the final analysis, did as much as Ritchie's goal to
take the teams into a third game at Hillsborough. Part three
of the Stoke–West Ham saga lacked goals but nothing else
and so it was on to Old Trafford where the automatic change
of referee saw me step into the act.

Conditions were appalling; clinging mud underfoot,

driving rain and wind. But the game before almost 50,000 spectators was packed from start to finish with drama, incident, excitement and good football.

The match was thirteen minutes old when the first piece of drama unfolded. West Ham goalkeeper Bobby Ferguson was injured diving courageously at the feet of the elusive Conroy and, after a seven minute hold up, he left the field dazed and concussed with West Ham electing to play on with ten men and Bobby Moore in goal.

Ron Greenwood, caught up in the tension of a Cup semi-final, accused Conroy of kicking Ferguson in the head when he could have withdrawn his boot and telly tried to sub-stantiate the claim. But it simply wasn't like that. It was a pure accident, the sort goalkeepers risk every playing day of their lives. Immediately Ferguson went down I ran across to Conroy and said: 'Don't worry. I saw what happened and it wasn't your fault. Forget it.' He needed to know that I understood.

West Ham were determined to get Ferguson back onto the park and Bobby Moore, dredging up all the experience of his World Cup days, was the man to hold the fort in the meantime. Young Clyde Best was their emergency keeper but at 20 years of age the sheer theatre of the occasion was too much for him and he asked to be relieved of his duties.

In the next twenty minutes I don't know if the greatest drama was on the field or beneath the stand where West Ham's backroom boys were working feverishly on Ferguson.

The excitement of the crowd reached a crescendo when stand-in Moore saved a penalty kick only for the rebound to be rapped smartly home to give Stoke the lead. McDowell had attempted to find Moore with a back pass but instead turned the ball into the path of Ritchie and then knocked the centre-forward over as he was going through.

Moore punched out Bernard's 12-yard shot but it went

straight back to the Stoke man who scored. The linesman flagged to indicate that two players had encroached into the penalty area before the kick was taken but the goal stood as West Ham were infringing and not Stoke.

Meanwhile, tucked away from 50,000 prying pairs of eyes, Ferguson was doing ball work with substitute Peter Eastoe in the corridor outside the dressing-rooms. He was catching the ball instinctively and shouting: 'Hit them harder' although he didn't know what he was saying. Ferguson had been sitting in the treatment room when there was a knock on the door and a polite inquiry about his health.

'Who are you?' he asked. 'I know your face but I don't know your name.' It was Bobby Charlton.

That sort of bravery isn't uncommon in our League but it is the very essence of our game. Surrender doesn't come easily.

West Ham were level at 1–1 thanks to a Billy Bonds 25-yarder flying in with the help of a deflection before Ferguson returned after an absence of twenty minutes; Brooking made it 2–1 with a stunning goal; and Peter Dobing dragged it back to two all. See-saw excitement . . . yet it was only after half-time and the two major flashpoints which were to be spotlighted by Jimmy Hill were still to come!

Five minutes after the restart Stoke went ahead again with what proved to be the winning goal. Lampard and Brooking between them lost the ball on the right and let in Marsh who centred. The ball was headed out to Conroy who beat Ferguson with a magnificent shot into the left hand corner of the West Ham net.

All straight-forward as far as I was concerned but not as far as television was concerned. Hill reckoned that at the moment Conroy struck the ball a Stoke player was standing offside and was interfering with play.

He also claimed a penalty for West Ham. Well, he had a point – there was a foul – but there was more to it than that. Geoff Hurst was obstructed by Alan Bloor but recovered to go on and cross the ball accurately for Harry Redknapp to strike the foot of a post when it was easier to score.

My point is this: did Jimmy Hill (or West Ham for that matter) prefer an indirect free-kick to the chance of a free shot from only eight yards? I mean, there were actually two attackers totally unmarked when the ball came over and I reckon two possible shots from eight yards is even better than one shot from twelve yards.

TV gave me the once over and, as sure as night follows day, letters came pouring in from West Ham supporters who blindly followed the Jimmy Hill line of reasoning. They accused me of just about every crime known to man. Stoke City officially complained about the programme and the Football League asked me to let them have all correspondence I'd received which I duly did. I never heard the outcome, of course, but perhaps Mr Hill heard something.

Really I don't feel a need to defend myself. The newspapers actually praised my overall performance at Old Trafford and the Daily Mirror printed the following comment piece:

'Jimmy Hill can be one of television's more irritating sports personalities. He "talked us through" a number of incidents in that magnificent Stoke–West Ham replay during ITV's "On the Ball" programme on Saturday.

'He reckoned that Alan Bloor's challenge on Geoff Hurst amounted to a penalty. But the action replay stopped there. It didn't show Hurst's recovery and cross into the middle from where Harry Redknapp shot against a post. Hasn't Jimmy Hill heard of the advantage rule?

'He said that the re-run showed conclusively that John Ritchie was offside at the moment when Terry Conroy struck Stoke's winning goal. He must have been watching a different replay to the one I saw because the pictures on my screen showed nothing of the sort. I'm not saying the camera lied. Just that to me the pictures didn't tell quite the same story as Jimmy Hill's version.'

While ITV searched for controversy the general feeling was that we had all witnessed a unique performance. Without doubt that was true of me. Many times I have been asked to name the greatest match I have ever refereed. People expect me to say the FA Cup final, world club championship or the like but I unswervingly pick this game – it had everything and a medal ought to be struck for every player who so brilliantly mastered the monsoon conditions.

Stoke City made Wembley this time only a year after they had failed in the FA Cup semi-final because of an injury-time penalty I awarded to Arsenal. You see how things even themselves out through time? One year I was a villain to Stoke supporters, the next an okay guy while it was the turn of West Ham's fans to stick pins in me. That's the way it goes in my job.

I was more than content with my performance at Old Trafford, right enough, but a month later it was a vastly different story in another cup-tie. This was at the Baseball Ground where Derby County were playing Arsenal and I had a shocker. I was slated by the Press and quite rightly so. I had to accept the criticism because it was deserved. The pitch was a mudheap and I tried to make allowances for the conditions with the result that I let far too much go and the game rapidly disintegrated.

Boy, the headlines were pearlers. 'Oh ref, what a disgrace' announced the Sunday Mirror and Frank McGhee went on to say : 'When the FA Cup causes players to behave as some from both sides did at Derby yesterday it makes one wonder whether even this trophy is worth it. The match was a disgrace to football and the remarkable tolerance of referee Pat Partridge is underlined by the fact that he booked only one player.'

The Sun, looking to the replay, said: 'They had better dig trenches and put up barbed wire at Highbury tomorrow. For these two teams gave a chilling demonstration of just how much they dislike each other and just how far they will go to prove it. Many people will demand a scapegoat for a match that in all truth made something of a mockery of the referees' clean-up campaign. The obvious one is Pat Partridge, a referee who apparently could neither see nor hear any evil.'

Brian Glanville, the Sunday Times scribe, referred to my 'eccentric refereeing' and after recalling a flare-up between George Graham and John O'Hare commented: 'If the new refereeing dispensation means anything at all, one or both should have gone straight off the field. Instead Mr Partridge, the referee, consulted his linesman, then reprimanded . . . Simpson and Gemmill. It reminded one of Max Miller's joke about the time he saw his wife kissing the milkman: "I went outside and I didn't half kick his horse." '

The Graham–O'Hare flashpoint was universally used to highlight my poor performance but what happened there was that I was following play and didn't see Graham, who fell under challenge from O'Hare, leap up and run at O'Hare for them both to begin antics which quickly attracted other players like bees round a honey pot. When I tried to unravel the mess in consultation with my linesman he had only seen Gemmill and Simpson making a few noises on the perimeter of the incident and, acting on the only evidence available, I demanded that they should cool it.

It was a typical case of a ref on a bad day not getting it

quite right yet striving to do his job and keep in touch.

The pitch was a heavy bog which meant that the ball was likely to stop while sliding limbs carried on and the conditions became exploited. The cynical after-match comment of Arsenal's Peter Storey – 'If you keep running with the ball in a match like that you know what to expect' – sadly summed up many attitudes and I failed to stamp on them.

If the world was temporarily against me then surprisingly I made a lasting friendship at the Baseball Ground – radio personality Pete Murray. I met Pete, a fervent Arsenal supporter, in the Derby car park prior to the game when he asked me if I knew a place to eat and, on his radio programme 'Open House' two days later, he recalled the meeting and ventured the opinion that I'd had a good game. He must have been the only person to think so.

Fortunately the game had ended in a draw two all and so I was given another chance to put things right in the replay at Highbury on the Tuesday afternoon. Bang on the doorstep of the Fleet Street Press who were no doubt waiting for me with their big knives.

There was no way I was going to make the same mistakes again and this time I hit everything hard and first time. There were three cautions with Alan Ball, John O'Hare and Alan Hinton the victims and, believe it or not, I was accused of being too strict only seventy-two hours after being told I was too soft!

Again there were no winners all round . . . neither me, Arsenal nor Derby County, the game before a capacity 63,000 ending o–o after extra time.

However as I dashed for my train from King's Cross with Newcastle United manager Joe Harvey and director Fenton Braithwaite, who had been at the game, I felt much happier with life. PP was back in control and, just to prove that we do bounce back, I went on to referee in the next round of the FA Cup, the sixth; take the Football League v Scottish League game at Ayresome Park; Scotland's international with Peru at Hampden and the FA Challenge Trophy final at Wembley.

A terrible season, wasn't it?

13   Abroad

I 've refereed in India where they put a steam-roller on the pitch at half-time to flatten it and in Malta where the glare off the white sand could almost blind you. I've been to Corsica, the historic land of bandits where fireworks lit up the night sky in a display never bettered on November 5 and to Japan where Tokyo University made a graphic study of my every move.

I've refereed the one and only Pele in Brazil; his team-mates Jairzinho, Rivelino and Paulo Cesar; super Germans Beckenbauer, Sepp Maier and Gerd Muller; Eusebio and Cruyff; and a side called Dynamo Kiev which was good enough to become the Russian national team en bloc.

And I've been slap bang in the middle of a referees' strike in Kuwait. Hardly a boring life, really!

If travel broadens the mind then football has been more than good to me . . . I've spent ten weeks in Kuwait, a month in Brazil, three weeks in Japan, fifteen days in Qatar in the Middle East, and a fortnight in India. Those are long trips but memorable ones and I've never even mentioned the World Cup finals in Argentina.

Kuwait was unique if only for that strike. It all began one Sunday when I was invited to a party in the Association offices. A party in a dry state like Kuwait meant tea and soft drinks but everyone who was anyone was there in their best bib and tucker. It transpired that three of their international referees were getting their white FIFA badges which was quite something. You've got to do two full internationals after getting on the FIFA list before you qualify for a white badge and in this country that can take up to five or six years but with all the tournaments held in the Middle East it's a much simpler and quicker process.

Nonetheless it was a proud moment and I remember wishing it was me up there in the spotlight. I was a FIFA referee at the time (late 1973) but hadn't yet been awarded my white badge. Appropriately mine was to eventually be presented at a Referees' Association conference in Gateshead not a corner kick away from my home.

The following Tuesday after the little party I was to run the line at a game where two of my newly-elevated friends were officiating with me. The Arabs were always somewhat lax when it came to punctuality and during my stay in Kuwait I became known as 'the Englishman who starts on time' which evidently was something of a novelty. A limousine with chauffeur was always at my disposal and we would often arrive at a ground before it was even open and have to sit outside waiting. The other match officials would turn up a quarter of an hour before the scheduled kick-off. So it was on this occasion.

The crowds were pouring in and the television cameras were going up in readiness for the game. Both managers had written out their team sheets and it was all systems go . . . except that I was sitting alone in the referee's dressing-room wondering what on earth to do with my flag!

The other linesman, who was chairman of the Referees' Committee, eventually walked in and said: 'There's no game today.' Before I could utter a word the referee, who had also got his badge two days earlier and was the committee secretary, arrived and explained: 'We're on strike.'

Ever had the feeling that the ceiling had fallen in on you? Well, that's how I felt.

My first reaction was 'my God, they've ganged up on me.' I'd been refereeing nearly all the big matches and felt that the locals might resent the intrusion. But no, I was assured the strike had nothing to do with me. It was an old grievance left over from the previous season which was still unresolved. Now my panic switched to the reaction of the crowd when they were told there was no game. Around 16,000 spectators were packed into the stadium and the telly boys were ready to record every precious moment. Can you imagine what would happen in England on a Saturday afternoon if the fans were told just before the kick-off that the match was cancelled because the ref had gone on strike? I doubt if much of the stadium would be left to sweep up.

I pleaded with the two lads to change their mind arguing that they had made their point and proved they could stop a game but it all fell on deaf ears. The lack of response from our dressing-room must have filtered along the corridor because in came the president of the Kuwait FA and all three started going at each other hammer and tongs in Arabic. I excused myself and sat outside, still in my black and white gear, while the voices became more raised and more angry.

No one could budge the two FIFA referees. Not even the president. The match was off.

Almost as incredible as the strike was the immediate reaction to it. The crowd simply filed away and the television crew packed its gear and left. One or two supporters who by now had got to know me shouted jocularly: 'Come on Mr Patrick, referee the game for us' but there was no violence, no angry scenes. Nothing.

The following day there was a meeting of the FA Council and on the Thursday the two who had received their FIFA badges at an official ceremony the previous Sunday were kicked out of football. A sharp, swift way to put down a strike.

What a hectic ten-week tour it was. I refereed fifteen games and ran the line in another, did a nine-session course for thirty-odd referees plus six lectures of their established refs, and assessed their referees in twenty-one matches. But the joy was that once Arabs take to you they will trust you with their lives and I was given the very best of treatment. A typical example was the day I complained of a sore throat and fifteen minutes later was being examined by the top throat specialist in the country, a European.

They played their football on hard-baked sand pitches similar to the one I'd encountered in Malta a couple of weeks before flying to Kuwait and the standard wasn't bad. To master the conditions a player had to be skilful and not physical and they were. Another point – the discipline was first rate. There was no badgering of referees.

Japan was totally different to Kuwait but equally as intriguing. I flew there on tour with Coventry City (the Japanese FA had requested that a referee should accompany the party) and took charge of a few games including the Keio Univ v Wasenda Univ match which is the equivalent to our Oxford v Cambridge varsity game at Wembley. At the toss up the two teams exchanged pennants and I admired them in passing. A few days later two similar silk pennants arrived at my hotel . . . a nice touch.

It was during this game that I came under the scientific eye of Tokyo University. Mr Toshio Asami, associate professor of the University and a prominent FIFA referee in Japan, was doing a survey to estimate the appropriate distance covered by a referee in a match with a view to devising a suitable method of training for physical fitness.

An eight-man team closely monitored three referees and three players to give a clearer overall picture and I was sent a copy of the full written report plus graphs. It materialised that I covered 10,800 metres or 6.75 miles during the varsity game compared to 6.5 miles by another English referee, Norman Burtenshaw, when he took Spurs v Japan out there.

Top man was Dukla Prague's linkman Masopust with 7.75 miles. Eusebio did 6.2 miles and a local Japanese striker called Kamamoto only 4.5 miles. I'm not sure what it all proved but I've told Norman Burtenshaw that it means I'm the most travelled ref in the country!

Tours are great for seeing places and spectacles you would probably otherwise never get the opportunity to see and Japan was no exception. Take Sumo, the traditional Japanese wrestling – you know, the big heavies who weigh about twenty-four stone, wear nothing but a belt around their waist and between their legs, and look about as cheerful as a gorilla with toothache.

I went with a friend, Chris MacDonald, to the Sumo wrestling and became totally addicted mainly because his knowledge of the complicated sport allowed me to appreciate what was going on. I sat glued to the television for the next two days watching the finals. I'm certain the Coventry lads thought I was mad.

Chris had the distinction of being the only non-Japanese to go into the ring for the hair cutting ceremony which is performed when a Sumo wrestler retires. Apparently once a boy had been selected to go to a Sumo stable and become a Sumo then his hair is not cut and he receives an allowance to have his hair set etc. Hence the ceremony when he retires.

My first meeting with Pele occurred on this tour though I didn't referee him until later when I spent a month in Brazil. The fascination of this man throughout the world was never more evident than in Tokyo. The Olympic

Stadium was full because he was playing and the Crown Prince and Princess completely broke with tradition to attend the game and meet the players, almost certainly because he was there. When Santos took the field they carried out their normal practice of holding aloft the Japanese flag and within a few moments the team was submerged by swarms of youngsters who tore the shirt off Pele, who had yet to kick a ball. I was sitting with some Japanese referees who told me it was the first time a football pitch had ever been invaded by young supporters.

Pele's response was typical . . . he scored two stunning goals in a 3–0 win for Santos. He was an unassuming man who never gave me an ounce of bother on the field despite being the target for the hatchet men who wanted to prevent him from playing. A credit to football without doubt.

Another club tour I was invited to undertake was Crook Town's visit to India in May of 1976. The little non-league side were bolstered by a few full-timers from the League like Irish international Eric McMordie, Hartlepool's Graham Richardson, and Darlington's Eric Young and Clive Nattrass. The Indians had asked if it was possible to get the English Cup final supervisor not having the faintest idea that I lived only twelve miles from Crook.

The centre piece of the tour was supposed to have been Bobby Charlton but he was unable to make it at the last moment having just returned from South Africa. His non-appearance bitterly disappointed the Indians who were anxious to meet England's World Cup hero though Terry Paine helped by flying out to guest in the last game.

The spectator response to the matches was nothing short of amazing. The first game was at Calcutta's famous Eden Garden ground, the setting of so many Test matches, and nearly 80,000 people turned up. The average 'gate' over six matches was 45,000 which, considering there wasn't a household name in the Crook team, was a real eye-opener. A household name – blimey, there wasn't even a First Division player on view but still they came climbing up trees and clambering over corrugated roofs to catch a glimpse of the action.

Eden Garden, India's answer to Lord's cricket ground, was some experience. We changed in a huge dressing-room partitioned off by screens with large fans whirring above our heads to bring relief from the stifling heat and cross-legged white-robed old men playing weird Indian music outside.

The ground itself has to be the best draining surface I've ever come across bar none. I found that out when I was asked to make a pitch inspection in a flood. I couldn't believe my ears . . . water was up to four inches deep in places and the car taking me to the Eden Garden had to crawl through mini lakes after a typical downpour. Conditions were perfect for water polo but football – it was ridiculous.

It seemed the daftest request I'd ever heard but to pacify our hosts I agreed to go along with it. We had to paddle through water lapping round our ankles to get from the enclosures onto the pitch but it was like a sponge absorbing the stuff at an astonishing rate. The ground had been totally submerged, now it was clear of surface water though extremely wet and heavy. It was the spectators who bothered me – the terracing was still awash.

However there were still a few hours to kick-off and my Indian friends implored me to forget about any diversions and concentrate purely on the pitch. If I felt it had a chance would I say so . . . never mind the water sloshing about elsewhere.

On the evidence of the recovery rate in such a short space of time I had to agree that some sort of miracle was possible. So the game was declared on. The only time I almost needed a rowing boat to get me out for a pitch inspection.

Sure enough, by the time we all returned for the match there wasn't a sign of water anywhere and we played in first-rate conditions with the fans dry and comfortable. What a country.

The humidity made it hard going, especially in the afternoons, and we Europeans suffered like nobody's business. The Indians perspired quicker than we did but they broke through the pain barrier and were okay. We copped it good and proper.

Because it was a tight tour (half a dozen games in a fortnight) it was agreed that Crook could not only field as many subs as they wished but could bring players back on again. That made sense in the conditions and was fine for the lads but what about the poor old ref? There was no rest for me, no sub limbering up on the touchline to give me a breather. I had to keep plodding on hoping I'd get my second, third or fourth wind. To say I came home shattered would be an understatement. I was like a Zombie.

One day I refused to ref. I wanted a rest like the players were getting but I was in charge of every single game. It came to a head when the tour organiser called into the hotel at ten o'clock at night and told me I was refereeing the next day. Not on your sweet life, I told him. It may have been a club tour with every game a friendly but I was still professional enough to want to prepare in the proper way and, besides, I was drained with the humidity. My legs were like lead.

It was all a bit much. The tour was supposed to be something of a holiday and I had taken Margaret with me so we could have a break but I wasn't seeing anything of a mystical country apart from the inside of Eden Garden.

Come match day the panic was there for all to witness. For some reason they didn't want one of the local boys handling the game yet I had FIFA refs running the line for me. It didn't make sense really.

When I left the hotel I had no gear with me and I could feel the sideways glances of officials. What's he up to? He hasn't got his grip, has he? The whispers and nudges grew but no one dare approach me and I kept mum. Margaret was following at a discreet distance . . . with my bag. But no one thought of checking with her.

In the dressing-room there were five blokes sitting around fidgeting uneasily. Two would be chosen as linesmen quarter of an hour before the kick-off. I plonked myself down beside them.

Despite the obvious amusing side with red-faced officials trying to contain their mounting panic I felt more angry than anything else. What a comic cuts way of running things. I relented, as I knew I always would, with twenty minutes to go but I told them: 'I hope you've learned your lesson. In England we don't treat referees like that.'

If organisation was somewhat lackadaisical in India then in the Iron Curtain countries it was spot on as you might imagine. I went to Russia to take the Dynamo Kiev–PSV Eindhoven European Cup-Winners' Cup semi-final in 1975 and the security was unbelievable. Evidently there had been a minor disturbance at a previous game and that was enough. There wasn't going to be a repetition, the law would see to that. The pitch was ringed by police sitting expressionless shoulder to shoulder in the front row of the seats. Needless to say there wasn't a peep from any would-be troublemakers.

During the game the ball spun out of play from a block tackle. It was one of those close decisions but I gave a corner against Kiev and their full-back, running to take up his position on the goal-line, said in perfect English: 'Your decision was perfectly correct, referee. It was a corner.' You could have knocked me down with a feather. 'Yes,' he smiled. 'I speak English. If you want any help please come and see me.'

That Kiev club side was also the full Russian national team at the time and they autographed the match ball for me after the game.

We've all read James Bond and had the pants scared off us by stories of sinister border guards in the East inviting us to 'come this way please.' Well, I've actually had a taste of it and lived to tell the tale.

I flew to Berlin for the East Germany v Turkey World Cup game and took a car through Checkpoint Charlie to Dresden in the East. There were quite a number of people in the queue for documentation but a guard looked quizzically at me.

'Mr Partridge?'

Nod.

'Referee?'

Nod.

'Come this way, please.'

I was ushered through. Preferential treatment, no less. But on the return journey it was ever so slightly different.

A guard checking my documents frowned, and glanced at a colleague who got the message and scuttled off to bring the head of security. He arrived, a big man with a bluff face.

'Do you want to keep us?' I inquired, indicating my two companions who were by now a lighter shade of pale.

'Yes, we have big rooms here,' he said with a nod towards a nearby door.

'With those on?' Handcuffs were plainly visible.

'If you require them.'

The twinkle in the eye indicated he was enjoying the

banter and I was warming to the theme. With a flourish he completed my forms (someone had forgot to sign something) and handed them back.

'I'm going now,' I said.

'And I'd keep going if I were you,' came the reply. We laughed – but didn't bother to look back as we went on through at a brisk pace!

The greatest club match a referee can officiate abroad is the world club championship – in theory at least. It's the match between the European Cup holders and the champions of South America for the undisputed title of the greatest team on earth.

On December 21, 1976 that match was mine . . . Bayern Munich of West Germany v Cruzeiro of Brazil in Belo Horizonte where Matthews, Mannion, Wright and the rest of the cream of English football had once suffered World Cup humiliation at the hands of the USA.

While the honour was undeniable luck was also involved and that's something I should like to see eliminated in the future. Let me explain.

If the game is in South America UEFA draw up a list of five officials and submit it to the South American federation who then select the final three. On this occasion the three were Robert Wurtz of France, Alberto Michelotti of Italy and me and we all flew to Brazil without having the faintest idea who would actually be in the middle on the big day. It's that indecision I would dearly like to see changed. It could lead to problems.

The way the referee is determined is quite ludicrous – lots are drawn an hour before kick-off. Dr Franchi, president of UEFA and chairman of the referees' committee of FIFA, came into our dressing-room at the appointed time and the Brazilians produced a bag with a black, red, and yellow ball in it. We were to pick a colour each and the lucky one was in business but Dr Franchi felt that was carrying things too far and, instead, wrote our three names on separate pieces of paper and drew one out himself. It was mine.

Fine. I was the winner. But that doesn't mean the system is right. It's not. The mental preparation of a referee for a world championship match cannot be right when he knows his fate depends on a lucky draw and, more important, the adverse effect bitter disappointment could have on someone only an hour before such a game is considerable. If a referee wasn't big enough to take it then everyone, including the players, would have a problem.

Luckily it didn't happen that way for me. I knew Robert Wurtz, we had been to Brazil together on a previous occasion, and he was superb about it. And though I didn't know Alberto Michelotti he took it in the right spirit as well.

As for the match itself I would like to put in a plug on its behalf.

The world club championship has come in for some shocking publicity. The Celtic punch-up in South America and Nobby Stiles being ordered off when Manchester United met Estudiantes in Brazil has given it a bad name over here. One English club actually refused to take part in it after winning the European Cup.

If I'd listened to all the stories I'd have been terrified to death. Blood and thunder and thuggery were words more associated with it than football.

My experience over the ninety minutes was the exact opposite. There wasn't even a yellow card shown in the whole game. All I had to do was have the odd word with the Brazilians, that's all.

And the talent on view was something special. Cruzeiro was the club of Brazil's brilliant World Cup striker Jairzinho and Bayern Munich included Beckenbauer, Maier, Schwarzenbeck, Hoeness and Muller.

Bayern had won the first leg 2–0 in West Germany and they lifted the trophy with a 0–0 draw in Brazil which only goes to show that the South Americans don't always resort to rioting when victory isn't theirs.

The elegant Beckenbauer was the architect of Bayern's success. He was everything to all that day. He made it all look so easy . . . a player of genuine quality.

14   Want to be a ref?

There's no way in which I could write a book and not at
some stage talk specifically to budding referees. They
are as much the lifeblood of the game as the players themselves and deserve all the encouragement they can get from
people like myself who have been fortunate enough to go
all the way.

It may even be that, having read my story, you wish to
take up refereeing for the first time. If that's so all you have
to do is to contact your local County Football Association
who will advise you as to where and when the next referees'
coaching course is being held.

The course, I feel, will open your eyes inasmuch as you
will be told there are seventeen laws to the game of
Association Football – yes, only seventeen – and also that
these laws are in fact universal. However, whether or not
they are applied universally is another matter. You'll be
surprised to read how simply worded these laws are and as
the course goes on you'll begin to think that anyone can
become a referee. Well, I believe that anyone with average
intelligence CAN pass a referee's examination which, incidentally, is the only exam a referee has to take throughout
his career. The failure rate is very low indeed.

But be warned – once having taken the course and passed
the examination you aren't a referee. All you have is a
certificate saying you know the laws of the game. Similar

to passing a driving test, it doesn't make you an advanced driver.

All referees have to go through this basic set-up starting out as a Class Three referee, which usually allows you to referee in the minor, youth and junior age group. Then if all goes well you are promoted to Class Two which is usually around the local works teams or similarly organised sides. If you can then prove that you are capable of making a further step up to Class One by your performances in front of County FA members, and assessors or advisers, then you have completed all classifications.

Throughout these steps you are also marked by the clubs on your performance on the field of play and, as I've already said, I can't argue that this is wrong. If clubs of any standing in any league look at the marking system properly they must agree that it's a way not only of helping a referee but in the long run helping to improve the efficiency of their league as well.

It may seem all too simple but, of course, refereeing a game of Association Football isn't as simple as all that.

If you have gained Class One status then no doubt you are ambitious and want to reach the top. This is the way it should be. We all must have a goal to aim for but don't over-reach too quickly. If you're given the opportunity to go further then grab it with both hands, keep your feet on the ground, and make the most of it progressing at the speed at which you have control, rather like driving a vehicle.

It should always be remembered that not all candidates can reach the top but don't stop trying which is where a lot of referees make their mistake. When they are not making the progress which they think they should be making, when they start to complain that other referees and not them-selves are climbing the ladder of success, what happens? Who do they blame? As often as not officialdom, the clubs, and even the system. It's never their own fault.

There are many pitfalls in this game and I believe that from the outset you must adopt a professional attitude, you must look at your performance after each game, be your own invigilator, and depending on your own intuitive thoughts of your immediate past ninety minutes, have a question and answer session with yourself.

You must ask: Could I have improved my performance? Where did I go wrong? Was my attitude towards the game correct? Could I have helped to make it a better game? Did I speak to players in the same manner I would expect to be spoken to?

In my opinion we have referees whose attitudes are totally wrong. When they go out to referee they think that they can't possibly make a mistake and they are prepared to jump down the throat of the first player who speaks to them. That's ridiculous. Downright stupid. Remember everyone is entitled to an opinion though how they express that opinion is what matters. The person who has never made a mistake hasn't been born yet.

One way in which referees could enjoy the game more is if from the outset of their career they trained hard and didn't wait until they gained promotion, say, to a league that uses neutral linesmen. Far too many make that mistake.

I'd like to dwell for a moment if I may on pre-match preparation. I believe it should begin when we receive an appointment. Let me clarify that statement. Be honest with yourselves for a moment – how often on receiving an appointment do you get that excited feeling inside? My own answer is nearly always. If I don't get a feeling of excitement I want to know the reason why.

On receiving an appointment, whether by post or phone, and no matter at what level, I think about the sort of game it will turn out to be. By doing this I believe it helps me approach every game with enthusiasm. We must bear in mind that each game we referee is very important not only to the players concerned but to ourselves.

No one game should be singled out for special treatment as far as training preparation goes e.g. why should you do an extra-half hour's training for a game one week and not bother with the extra training for the following week's game? Different divisions don't require different amounts of training – you have the same ingredients for every game and therefore the consistency should be equal. Only the mixing may be different.

I can't understand a referee who, because he has a cup final, suddenly feels a dire need to make an extra effort.

I concede the fact, of course, that if it's very cold on the day of the match you should do some extra warm-up exercises in the dressing-room prior to going out so that you look relaxed and not stiff and freezing.

A very important part of preparation is training. In fact it's top priority because if you have a healthy body then it should follow that your mind is also healthy. The amount of training we require depends on our occupation. For example a desk or car-bound person obviously needs to arrange to go training whereas the person who teaches physical exercise can incorporate his training into his daily routine.

There are many ways of getting the body tuned up but never fall into the trap of using the old excuse about lack of facilities for not training on a cold, wet and miserable night. There is always a road handy, and if you live in a block of flats, then there will almost certainly be flights of stairs you can run up and down. Indoors, you can always do isometrics even while watching television!

Squash, I find, is very helpful for reflex action. You can

join in with the local players or go to an evening college and join the PE class. If you're keen and willing there is always a way.

Fitness is an important part of the make-up of a referee, both mentally and physically. League assessors usually compliment me on this point at least and the day they need to criticise my fitness is the day I'll pack in.

What should you do the night before a match? Each one of us obviously differs from the other but whatever you do, do it in moderation. On the morning of the match you should try and relax. This is not always possible but do try and avoid tension, for example having an argument with someone, especially someone you think a lot about. This may have repercussions and could possibly impair your judgement during the game.

At a local match arrive in plenty of time, let the players and officials see that you are keen and on your toes. Don't arrive minutes before the kick-off and find you have no time left to sort out the last-minute problems. Your attitude in the dressing-room, even if you change with one or both teams, should always be cordial. Never be aloof.

Try hard to put the club linesman at ease, remember you want him to do you a service. It's easy to make enemies but more difficult to cement a friendship.

If you have the privilege of having neutral linesmen then make certain they are made to feel part of a team. In fact convince them they are part of a team which is going to be the best team on the field. If you're a linesman give all you've got to your colleague with the whistle because next time you're together the roles may be reversed and what is good to give cannot be bad to receive. Match preparation is not just preparing ourselves but helping to prepare our colleagues.

I have mentioned fitness in relation to referees and once

again I repeat, to be successful you must keep yourselves physically and mentally fit. There are many things which can be done to keep fit and I would like to suggest a few routines based on personal experience over the last few years.

In 1974 FIFA decided that any referee who was nominated to the international list must undergo what is called the Cooper Test. This is a test based simply on running over set distances in given times. For example referees between the ages of twenty-five and thirty-nine must cover a distance of 2,300 metres in twelve minutes to pass the test while referees between the ages of forty and fifty must cover at least 2,000 metres in twelve minutes. Then it's compulsory for all to do 400 metres in seventy-five seconds or less (this is the difficult one) followed by a fifty-metre sprint in eight seconds. The final physical test is 4 x 10 metres shuttles to be covered within 11.5 seconds. To top all that off a full medical has to take place which includes ECG, blood, water etc.

Last season the Football League introduced similar types of tests for the first time and, as in FIFA, if you were unable to complete the test then you weren't allowed to referee in the Football League. I'm all in favour of such tests having asked for them for some time. If we are going to compete in a professional game then we've got to be seen to be professional in our approach.

But whatever happens you should never over-do your training. If you have any problems during or after training for goodness sake consult a doctor.

Another fitness routine is as follows: To warm up start running for two or three minutes at a gentle pace, jog for a similar time, then walk, and start all over again keeping this up for ten to fifteen minutes after which your body will respond to more keener exercises.

After the warm-up period you should start doing some body exercises, press-ups and trunk bending. Once again I stress do not over-do it.

Your next period of training should be taken up by a five to six minutes run at a fair pace. Then do some shuttle running and go back to four or five minutes of running at a fair pace and shuttles again. Repeat this three or four times and finish off with a gentle run of 500 metres.

If you have to train on your own, and I know from experience it's hard, then don't cheat yourself. Adopt the attitude 'I'm going to better myself' and that should make you want to go on.

When you are training or refereeing you can get injured and if you do then get something done about it. Whatever you do please don't try and referee with pulled muscles or the like because if you do you run the risk of permanent injury. Get medical advice as quickly as possible.

Over the years I've been fortunate in my career with regard to training and medical advice. In my early days of refereeing I trained with the players at my local club Billingham Synthonia, even taking part in the seven-a-side games, and of course at the end of training if any treatment was required it was readily available.

Earlier in the book I've made reference to Middlesbrough FC who had done me proud over the years. Dr Neil Phillips, who is a director and of course has been the England team doctor, has given me lots of advice and has carried out my medical test in connection with FIFA. If I've been going to a foreign country for the first time Neil, as always, has been prepared to advise on jabs and what medication I should take with me. And if I've ever needed treatment I've been expertly looked after by a string of physios at Ayresome including George Wright, now with West Bromwich Albion; Jim Headrige, now with Bolton Wanderers; and Lew

Clayton. I'm extremely grateful to them all.

If you look in the dictionary the word 'referee' (which has seven letters) is described as 'One to whom a point or question is referred; a person to whom a matter in dispute is referred for settlement or decision, an arbitrator, an umpire.'

However, there's another seven-letter word which is frequently used towards referees. When I hear it I'm not offended because what those people may not realise is that they are paying me the finest compliment possible. That word is:

B – Brave
A – Adventurous
S – Solid
T – Tenacious
A – Audacious
R – Reliable
D – Disciplined

15   And so to work

INTRODUCTION

Professional footballers, particularly those in the First Division, lead a pampered existence on match weekends. If they are to travel then an army of help is on hand to make the arrangements and smooth the path . . . beginning with the club secretary booking the hotel and arranging transport in midweek, then the manager, coach and physiotherapist nursing them through the actual weekend tending to every need however small with the sole aim of relieving tension and apprehension before the big match kick-off. Even their food is ordered for them. All they have to do is find their way from home to the football ground where the team coach is parked.

But what of the referee? How does he prepare for a game where his split-second judgement and courage can determine where the season's top honours go? To find out how the other half live John Gibson travelled with Pat Partridge to Villa Park for last season's FA Cup semi-final between Arsenal and Wolves living with him through the twenty-four hours of build-up, the game itself, and the inevitable after-match inquests.

●   ●   ●

It was two thirty on a Friday afternoon and Pat Partridge

was loading his car in the front drive – a grip containing his neatly folded and laundered referee's gear and boots, an overnight bag for his wife Margaret, and a smart match-day suit in a zip-up hung above the back seat. Everything normal.

There's no such thing as a home game for a referee. Unlike a player who, on average, spends once a fortnight off the road Pat meticulously goes through his own highly-personalised travelling routine virtually every weekend. He must, by nature of his job, be a loner when it comes to matches. His 'team' is scattered and doesn't travel together but meets at the ground itself.

This week was par for the course. Semi-final or not, the demands of everyday life remain unswerving and Pat had been at work by seven o'clock in the morning mucking out and feeding the cows.

Now, however, farming was to be put aside for the weekend. The road ahead pointed to Villa Park, a capacity crowd, and the hardest match of all when dreams are either at last realised amid tremendous emotion or cruelly smashed at the last hurdle.

Margaret, as always, had made all the arrangements booking the hotel in consultation with Pat. The idea was to break the back of the 200-odd mile journey and stay at the Crest Motel in Walsall which was close enough to the ground if an early-morning pitch inspection became necessary.

Villa secretary Alan Bennett, handling his last match before taking up a similar appointment at Leicester, had phoned to say there were no immediate problems despite a downpour in the last twenty-four hours. But an eight o'clock call would be made to our hotel the following morning if necessary.

Reg Paine of the Football Association was more perturbed.

The weather had decimated soccer for three months causing the most catastrophic build up of games postponed through snow, ice and finally floods and the North East of England had been by far the worst hit. Only twelve days previously Pat had been unable to get out of his isolated farm to referee the sixth round match between Southampton and Arsenal at the Dell. A national newspaper had even tried to arrange a dramatic air lift with an RAF helicopter to get him out of ten-foot snow drifts but to no avail.

Since then floods had swept the area swollen by the melting mountains of snow and lashing rain.

'Get out – I don't care how many overnight stays it costs us,' was the FA message. And get out we did through flooded fields and country roads until, as the miles were eaten up, conditions became significantly better.

Players while away their time on journeys either by playing cards on the special tables in the middle of the luxury coaches or stretching out full length for a snooze. Pat drives himself. He's an advanced driver and prefers to take the wheel rather than be chauffeured. It enables him to relax and takes his mind off the game.

He eats sweets incessantly on a journey. Hard-boiled fruits sucked, not bitten. Yet he never eats a sweet at any other time. Ask him why and he shrugs. It's the same sort of trait as that which sees him drink gallons of tea at the ground prior to kick-off when, at home, he is strictly a coffee man. Habit-forming, it makes him feel at ease and that's what match build-up is all about.

Conversation was light, repeatedly returning to football. He reflected how, if the snow hadn't made him a prisoner on his own farm, handling Arsenal in the sixth round would have automatically precluded him from this particular semi-final. 'There's always a silver lining,' he smiled.

As it was this was to be Pat's fifth FA Cup semi-final and

he's had five in the League Cup as well plus three in European competitions. The others – Arsenal v Stoke at Hillsborough, Leeds v Wolves at Maine Road and Southampton v
Crystal Palace and Arsenal v Orient at Stamford Bridge –
each produced a memory related with instant recall and
punctuated only by the constant switching on of the car
radio every half hour to catch the sports news. 'Brady,
Young and Talbot have passed fitness tests for Arsenal,
Wolves pick from thirteen,' we were told.

A four-hour trip saw us arrive at the Crest Motel in the
shadow of Walsall's Fellows Park. New territory these days
for Pat Partridge since the Football League brought in a
system of regionalisation for their referees. Now Pat ven-
tures south only as far as Nottingham, Leicester or Derby
though the Football Association know no such boundary
restrictions for their cup-ties.

The Arsenal party were housed across the teeming concrete of Birmingham in the Holiday Inn but official and
contestants weren't being deliberately kept apart. Often,
purely by accident, Pat spends match night in the same
hotel as the visiting team. He doesn't believe in checking up
to see who else may be staying or prescribe to the belief
that confrontation brings embarrassment.

The receptionist was asked politely if the room was on the
quiet side of the hotel – a good night's sleep is essential to
a good performance the following day. Travel expenses plus
hotel accommodation are paid for by the FA in the case of
cup-ties but Pat must naturally pay for his wife who is a
constant traveller with him and gives rock-like support.
Margaret is an essential part of the Pat Partridge success
story.

Where a ref can score over a player is that, should he so
desire, he can take his wife with him on matches. Such a
thing is strictly forbidden by the clubs, of course, who even

on such big occasions as semi-finals insist upon the wives travelling separately and not seeing their husbands until after the game.

Players are told what to do, referees tell themselves. They are on trust and in Pat's case that's no problem. Moderation is his key word.

A quiet dinner (main course, cheese board and a glass of wine) was interrupted only to secure a bone for Tina back home. Ceremoniously kept in the fridge overnight and presented, gift wrapped, the next day before we left!

Top referees are recognised just like players and the inevitable request for an autograph came from a bright-eyed young lad called Rup who added the rider: 'You will let Wolves win, won't you?' A flashing smile accompanied the answer probably given a thousand times in such a situation: 'If they score the most goals they can win.'

What was significant throughout the entire weekend, or at least until after the match, was that Pat talked football enthusiastically and readily but never once discussed the game he was about to control. It was as though everyone knew the subject was taboo.

He was in bed before eleven o'clock, up before 9am and into the restaurant for breakfast dressed in a smart grey suit with FA badge on the pocket and FA tie. Every inch the ambassador.

From now on in the preparation of the referee and the players – central characters in an hour-and-a-half drama that afternoon – varies considerably. Players lie in bed until almost twelve noon when a meal is specially laid on for them, usually before the restaurant is open to the general public. They then have a team-talk and leave for the ground between one o'clock and two depending on the distance to be travelled.

Referees have no such luxury during the countdown to

kick-off. Pat's big meal is before the restaurant stops serving
breakfast which means he must be out of bed, dressed and
downstairs before nine thirty. He has the lot – mixed grill
with lashings of toast and preserves and several cups of
coffee.

The need to be on the spot in case of emergencies saw
us arrive at Villa Park by 11.30am which was more than
three hours before the action began and while most of the
players were only thinking of getting out of bed. The first
person we bumped into was John Motson, BBC TV commentator who, like us, needed an early start.

The games to be covered on Match of the Day every
Saturday night are a heavily guarded secret which, if
revealed publicly, can see the cameras switched to another
game. The secrecy is to protect the live gate, especially in
ordinary League games. If the fans knew in advance that
certain matches were on the box that night they wouldn't
bother turning up.

But Pat had known for a while that this particular semi
was the one to be featured on Match of the Day and we
had, in fact, checked the time of transmission to see if we
could watch the programme. As it was we could – the Euro-.
vision Song Contest had pushed the football back to a late
slot at 11.20 pm which suited us fine if nobody else.

Inside Villa Park's massive complex the pre-match buzz
was just beginning. Dozens of policemen were lined up in
the car park receiving their orders before being dispersed
to control a capacity crowd. There were to be fifty-six
arrests during the afternoon.

The telly people were meticulously checking their
equipment over and over again and the Villa stewards were
hurrying to their posts.

After checking in with secretary Alan Bennett we made
our way to the dressing-rooms. The ref's, still locked, was

quickly opened by an official who became even more flustered when Pat told him: 'I'd change the Wolves' sign if I were you – it's on the boot room.' Wolves had the home dressing-room across the corridor and Arsenal the away dressing-room on the right but someone had pinned the card saying 'Wolves' on the wrong door. The thought of Villa making their Midlands rivals change for a semi-final in the boot room appealed to my sense of humour.

Pat was out on the pitch by 11.45 taking a close look at conditions. 'It'll cut up,' he said. 'No doubt about that.' John Motson came over . . . he was on the air inside the next hour doing a live preview for Grandstand and was obviously perturbed.

'I've got a story,' he told us, 'only Arsenal won't confirm it. I'm certain Liam Brady isn't playing. Positive. The trouble is Terry Neill's keeping mum.' Semi-final day was living up to its reputation for drama. All the morning papers had forecast Brady would play. Now, even as the Arsenal supporters began to filter onto the huge embankment away to our right, came the first indications of a major surprise. Their best player was likely to miss out.

Villa president Trevor Gill, plainly delighted to see Pat, collared him on his return up the tunnel and whisked him away on a tour of Villa's superb amenities including underground restaurant and luxury boxes in the new stand. Coffee and sandwiches were booked in the vice presidents' lounge for one o'clock by which time Pat's team was all assembled . . . linesmen Stephen Bates and Frank Phipps and reserve official Malcolm Heath. When the semi-final stage is reached a reserve linesman is appointed and he gets changed in readiness for accidents. A sub, if you like.

The real business was about to begin. A short period of relaxation on the bench in the dressing-room letting every thought drain from the mind bar the match ahead, incessant cups of tea, a talk with colleagues on what is expected from them, change into kit as late as possible, and then warm-up exercises.

'I don't tell my linesmen what blade of grass to stand on,' says Pat. 'I want them to work for me – I want to use them, not have them for ornaments. They are a crucial part of a team and I want instant response. If they have to think "What did he say?" then we're all lost.'

Arsenal, without Brady to balance their left-hand side of the field, took the game cautiously to Wolves in the first-half almost like a fighter waiting to see the armoury ranged against him. They carried more class befitting a team nearer the top of the First Division, Wolves relying on the enthusiasm and organisation which had helped them out of the relegation cellar since the arrival of manager John Barnwell.

Where Wolves showed their naïvety was in the way strikers Billy Rafferty and John Richards repeatedly strayed into Arsenal's offside trap. There was more whistle for that than almost anything else.

Pat ran the show with quiet and complete efficiency. It was an easy game by semi-final standards producing the need for a word with offending players only on the odd occasion . . when Talbot, faced with a three-against-two situation, dropped his man; Young, up for an Arsenal corner, held the keeper as the ball was floated into a packed goalmouth; and O'Leary produced a clumsy touchline tackle on Richards.

Apart from offsides there were only thirteen free-kicks awarded against Wolves in the entire match and seventeen against Arsenal.

One decision, not big and quickly forgotten, underlined the class and experience of a master craftsman at work. Late in the first-half big Willie Young rose powerfully for a high ball pumped into the Arsenal penalty area and ended up falling all over Rafferty amid screams for a penalty from the Wolves contingent in the crowd. It looked bad to the uneducated. Willie is enthusiastic, gangling, and not the prettiest of players. A less experienced ref, or one without such a quick eye, might have taken the incident at face value. But Pat Partridge waved play on. He had seen Rafferty 'making a back' for Young as the ball was played in, that is quietly backing into an opponent who is beginning his jump. The clearance was true and Arsenal had the advantage. Both Young and Rafferty knew precisely what had happened. Rafferty merely walked away and Young picked himself up to applaud the decision and make a thumbs-up sign towards the referee. It's such moments which build up a reputation among hardened pro's.

Arsenal, the slumbering giants, stirred themselves in fifty minutes to snatch the lead. Daley lost the ball to Price who shrugged off a tackle from Carr and stroked the ball forward into the path of Stapleton at inside-right. Stapleton, by far the game's outstanding forward, suddenly accelerated to leave Wolves defenders stricken and whip a low, vicious shot across Bradshaw and into the far corner of the net.

'It was a brilliant goal made out of nothing,' Pat said later. 'When the ball was played up to Stapleton there was nothing on but he created space and opportunity. Until that moment I was convinced I was bound for White Hart Lane for a replay the following Wednesday. However there was only one winner after that. Too many Wolves heads dropped. It was as though they had lost belief in themselves.'

A second goal was always on the cards and it came in the seventy-ninth minute, ironically just as Wolves made their final fling sending on substitute Patching for Palmer. A soaring kick out of his hands by Jennings was missed by Berry and Sunderland was onto it hungrily to flick the ball round McAlle and push it cheekily through the legs of Bradshaw as the keeper advanced. That was it – 2–0.

To be truthful it was never a classical game nor a nerve-tingling one. The best team won which is perhaps amply illustrated by the fact that Wolves' only direct shot came from their sub, Patching, six minutes from time when Jennings made a brilliant reflex save tipping the ball over the bar with his wrong hand.

The moment must have reminded Arsenal that a Wembley appearance could yet be snatched from them because Jennings, lying at the feet of Partridge after the save, looked up and inquired: 'What time is it ref?'

'Twenty to five,' came the snappy reply. A perplexed Jennings thought for a couple of seconds then ventured: 'No, ref, I mean how long to go?'

'About five minutes,' said Pat, 'if you get up now and stop wasting time!' Jennings was on his feet in a flash.

The final whistle in a semi is either a joy to hear or the moment when the world caves in. After so many such occasions Pat Partridge is only too aware of the emotional extremes he evokes in that moment which is why he waited in the tunnel for one man – Wolves coloured defender George Berry.

'Okay, he made a mistake for their second goal but he's a young player who has a lot of quality,' said Pat. 'He was my man of the match and I wanted to let him know, in what was a dreadful moment for him, that I admired his performance.

'There was one tackle in particular which stood out in my memory. An Arsenal forward was through and lengthening his stride into the penalty area when Berry came across like greased lightning and took him out. Arsenal looked for a penalty but there was no way. The tackle was as clean as a whistle. I turned to Wolves skipper Kenny Hibbitt and said "That's some player." He nodded in agreement.'

Before Pat could climb into the bath for a long soak with a whisky and dry in his hand the dressing-room door was opened. It was John Barnwell, manager of the losers. 'Thanks for a good game, Pat,' he said. 'You did grand.'

It took a man to do that only minutes after losing a Cup semi-final and Pat appreciated the effort. 'Those few words meant more than if the whole of the Arsenal players had lined up to say thanks.'

Throughout the weekend my lasting impression of Pat Partridge was of a total lack of nerves, at least outwardly. For the first time that now changed. He became a compulsive talker. It's a means of unwinding which is totally under-standable. A good job of work done, the time had come for relaxing in the social atmosphere of soccer.

Wolves were magnificent in defeat. Their chairman Harry Marshall and director Gerry Devine joked with Pat and Margaret about getting a new suit apiece especially to meet the Partridges (an in-joke dating back a couple of seasons). 'We knew we'd no chance when we heard who was reffing,' kidded Mr Devine then, out of Pat's earshot, he confided: 'I wouldn't tell him but he had a good game, didn't he? We've no complaints there.'

Jack Taylor, employed as the commercial manager of Wolves, talked of the emotional pain of retirement.

'It hurts more than even I expected. I now realise it was $99\frac{3}{4}$ per cent of my life and even being involved with a League club isn't any compensation. The ironic thing is the older you get the easier it is to referee. Players have learned to respect you over the years and it shows in their reactions. Look at Pat today.'

Assistant manager Richie Barker, gathering his clan to-gether for the short, sad trip across country, stuck his head into the company to say: 'A nice friendly match eh? Too flippin' friendly from our point of view.'

Arsenal, of course, were in a much greater rush with a longer journey home but both Terry Neill and Don Howe took time out to shake hands as the chat went on unabated. FA councillors abound on semi-final day and all knew Pat and wanted to discuss various aspects of coaching referees or administration.

Jack Wiseman, Birmingham City's director who is also on the League Management Committee and FA Council, eventually spirited him into a corner for a final tête-à-tête before we set off home.

There are those who see a referee as a leper, someone to avoid with a nervous cough and a rapid exit line. But Pat Partridge has broken down a lot of those barriers among players, among managers and among directors. Ask George Berry, John Barnwell and Jack Wiseman.

I can't think of a better epitaph than that.